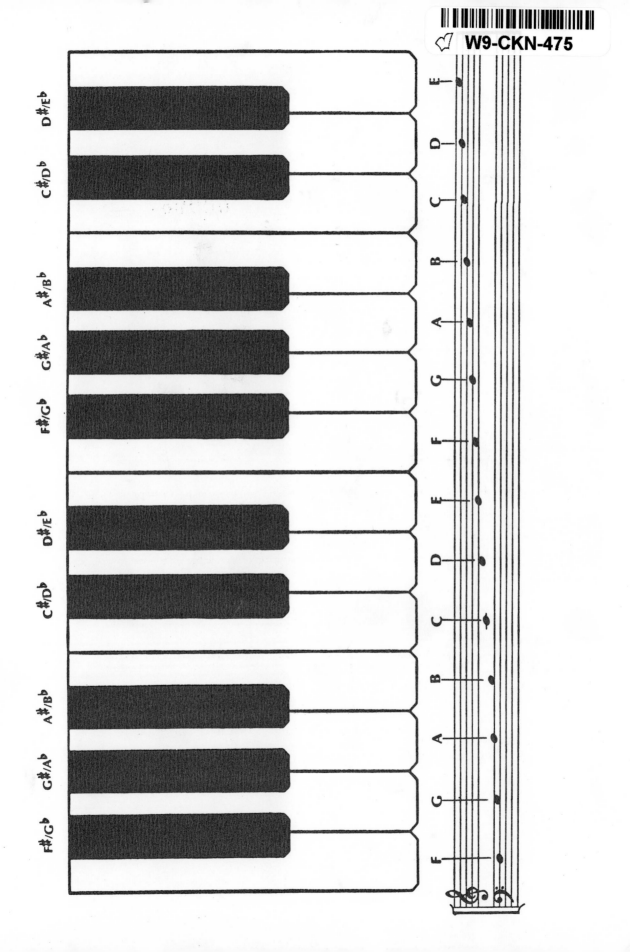

World of MUSIC

Jane Beethoven • Jennifer Davidson
Catherine Nadon-Gabrion
Authors

Carmino Ravosa • Phyllis Weikart
Theme Musical   Movement

Darrell Bledsoe
Producer, Vocal Recordings

Silver Burdett & Ginn
Morristown, NJ • Needham, MA
Atlanta, GA • Cincinnati, OH • Dallas, TX • Menlo Park, CA • Deerfield, IL

ISBN 0-382-07048-8

Contents

Sharing Music   160

THEME MUSICAL – ONLY LOVE IS SPOKEN HERE   190

Sing and Celebrate   208

Reference Bank   252

MUSIC FOR LIVING

Making New Friends

Getting to Know You

(from The King and I)

Words by Oscar Hammerstein II   Music by Richard Rodgers

Get-ting to know you, get-ting to know all a-bout you,

Get-ting to like you, get-ting to hope you like me.

Get-ting to know you, put-ting it my way, but nice - ly,

You are pre-cise - ly my cup of tea!

Get-ting to know you, get-ting to feel free and eas - y

When I am with you get-ting to know what to say.

Have-n't you no - ticed? Sud-den-ly I'm bright and breez - y

Be - cause of all the beau - ti - ful and new

things I'm learn-ing a-bout you day by day. _____

Other Children

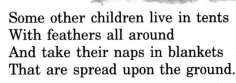

Some children live in palaces
Behind an iron gate
And go to sleep in beds of gold
Whenever it gets late.

Some other children live in tents
With feathers all around
And take their naps in blankets
That are spread upon the ground.

And way up north the children live
In houses built of ice
And think that beds made out of fur
Are really very nice.

In countries where the nights are hot,
Without a single breeze,
The children sleep on bamboo beds
That fasten in the trees.

Some day I think I'll travel 'round
And visit every land
And learn to speak the language that
Each child can understand.

They'll teach me how to play their games
And, if they want me to,
I'll show them different kinds of tricks
That I know how to do.

They'll want to ask me questions then
And I will ask them others,
Until at last we understand
Like sisters and like brothers.

Helen Wing

5

Echoes

Have you ever heard
your own echo? Where?
Try different ways of being
someone else's echo.

I Love Music

Words and Music by Carmino Ravosa

(ECHO)

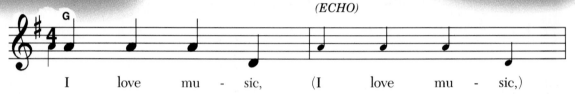

I love mu - sic, (I love mu - sic,)

An - y kind of mu - sic, (An - y kind of mu - sic,)

An - y kind of mu - sic, I love.
(An - y kind of mu - sic,) (I love.)

I love mu - sic, (I love mu - sic,)

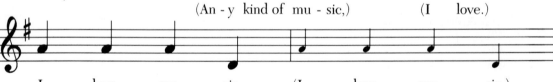

An - y kind of mu - sic, (An - y kind of mu - sic,)

An - y kind of mu - sic, I love.
(An - y kind of mu - sic,) (I love.)

Bird Talk

Can you imagine a bat or a bird talking?

Do a pat-clap pattern in time to the lively music of this nonsense song.

Pat clap, Pat clap

Leatherwing Bat

Traditional

1. "Hi," said the lit - tle   lea-ther-wing bat,   "I'll tell you   the rea - son that,

The rea - son that   I   fly by night Is be-cause I   lost   my heart's de-light."

REFRAIN

How - dy, dow - dy   did-dle - o - day,   How - dy, dow - dy   did-dle - o - day,

How - dy, dow - dy   did-dle - o - day,   How - dy, dow - dy   did-dle - o - day.

8

2. "Hi," said the blackbird, sitting on a chair,
    "Once I courted a lady fair;
    She proved fickle and turned her back,
    And ever since then I've dressed in black." *(Refrain)*

3. "Hi," said the woodpecker, sitting in the grass,
    "Once I courted a bonny lass;
    She proved fickle and from me fled,
    And ever since then my head's been red." *(Refrain)*

4. "Hi," said the greenfinch as he flew,
    "I loved one that proved untrue;
    And since she will no more be seen,
    Every spring I change to green." *(Refrain)*

Make up another verse for this song. Which bird or animal
will you sing about?

What do you think beetles, bugs, and bees would talk
about?

Little Talk

Don't you think it's probable
that beetles, bugs, and bees
talk about a lot of things—
you know, such things as these:

The kind of weather where they live
in jungles tall with grass
and earthquakes in their villages
whenever people pass!

Of course, you'll never know if bugs
talk very much at all,
because our ears are far too big
for talk that is so small.

Aileen Fisher

The Story of a Clock

Play a steady "tick-tock" pattern on your knees as you listen to this old song about a clock.

Tick-tock, tick-tock; Tick-tock, tick-tock.

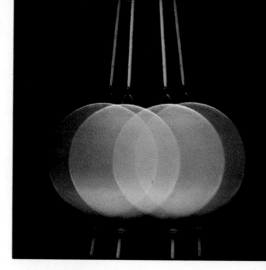

Grandfather's Clock

Words and Music by Henry C. Work

1. My grand - fa - ther's clock was too large for the shelf, So it
2. In watch - ing its pen - du - lum swing to and fro, Man - y

stood nine - ty years on the floor; _____ It was
hours had he spent while a boy; _____ And in

tall - er by half than the old man him - self, Tho' it
child - hood and man - hood the clock seemed to know, And to

weighed not a pen - ny - weight more. _____ It was
share both his grief and his joy. _____ For it

bought on the morn of the day that he was born, And was
struck twen - ty - four when he en - tered at the door, With a

10

al - ways his treas - ure and pride; But it
bloom - ing and beau - ti - ful bride; But it

stopped short, nev-er to go a-gain, When the old man died.
stopped short, nev-er to go a-gain, When the old man died.

REFRAIN

Nine - ty years with-out slum-ber - ing. tick - tock, tick - tock, His

life sec - onds num-ber - ing, tick - tock, tick - tock, It

stopped short, nev-er to go a-gain, When the old man died.

Parts for Percussion

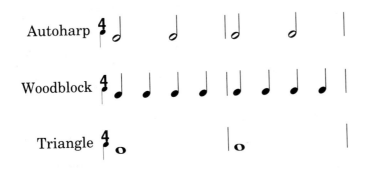

Autoharp

Woodblock

Triangle

What happens to the sound of the clock in this piece for orchestra by Leroy Anderson?

Syncopated Clock .... **Anderson**

11

A Toe-Tapping Melody

This cheerful, light-hearted song was composed by Stephen Foster. Clap or tap the beat as you listen to the music. Join in on the *some-folks-do* parts when you can.

Some Folks

Words and Music by Stephen Foster

1. Some folks like to sigh, Some folks do, some folks do;

Some folks long to cry, But that's not me nor you,

REFRAIN

Long live the mer-ry, mer-ry heart That laughs by night and day,

Like the Queen of Mirth, No mat-ter what some folks say.

2. Some folks fear to smile,
   Some folks do, some folks do;
   Others laugh through guile,
   But that's not me nor you. *Refrain*

3. Some folks get gray hairs,
   Some folks do, some folks do;
   Brooding o'er their cares,
   But that's not me nor you. *Refrain*

Play a Part

You can play the *some-folks-do* parts on the bells. Which
bells will you need?

B♭   G   A   F

**Stephen Collins
Foster**
(1826–1864)

Stephen Foster was born in Lawrence-
ville, Pennsylvania, on the Fourth of
July, 1826. Even as a little boy, he
showed an interest in music. When Stephen was two years old he could pick out
melodies on his sister's guitar. By the
time he was eight he could play the flute.
One of his first compositions was a piece
for four flutes.

Foster is remembered by some people as
America's favorite "folk-song" writer.
During his lifetime his melodies became
popular with people all over the United
States. Today some of Foster's songs are
known and loved in all parts of the
world.

"Some Folks" is one of the more than 200
compositions that Foster wrote.

Stephen Foster's Hit Song

The banjo was a popular folk instrument in Stephen Foster's time. Listen for its sound on this recording of "Oh, Susanna."

Oh, Susanna

Words and Music by Stephen Foster

I ___ came from Al - a - ba - ma With my ban - jo on my knee,

I'm ___ going to Loui - si - an - a, My ___ true love for to see;

It __ rained all night the day I left, The weath-er it was dry;

The __ sun so hot I froze to death; Su - san - na, don't you cry.

REFRAIN

Oh, Su - san - na, Oh, don't you cry for me,

I've __ come from Al - a - ba - ma With my ban - jo on my knee.

2. I had a dream the other night,
When ev'rything was still.
I thought I saw Susanna
A-coming down the hill.
The buckwheat cake was in her mouth,
The tear was in her eye.
Says I, "I'm coming from the South,
Susanna, don't you cry." *Refrain*

Of all the songs Stephen Foster wrote, "Oh, Susanna" is the best-known and best-loved. Foster wrote "Oh, Susanna" for a small singing society that he conducted. Later it became the favorite song of the "forty-niners" when they traveled to California's goldfields.

On this recording you will hear two different singing groups performing "Oh, Susanna" in two different styles.

"Oh, Susanna" . . . . The Byrds

"Oh, Susanna" . . . . The Mormon Tabernacle Choir

A Southern Banjo Tune

It's easy to feel the beat in this cheerful song about Cindy.
Listen for the sound of the banjo in the recording and keep
the beat in your own way.

Cindy

Southern Banjo Tune

(A) 1. I wish I was an ap - ple, A - hang - in' on a tree;
2. She took me to her par - lor, She cooled me with her fan,

And ev - 'ry time my Cin - dy passed She'd take a bite of me.
She swore I was the pur - tiest thing in the shape of mor - tal man.

You ought to see my Cin - dy, She lives a - way down South;
I wish I had a nee - dle, As fine as I could sew,

She is so sweet the hon - ey bees All swarm a - round her mouth.
I'd sew that gal to my coat - tail, And down the road I'd go.

(B) **REFRAIN**

Get a - long home, Cin - dy, Cin - dy, Get a - long home, Cin - dy, Cin - dy,

Get a - long home, Cin - dy, Cin - dy, I'll mar - ry you some day.

Add a Part

Here are two harmony parts you can use with the refrain
(section B) of the song.

Descant

Get a - long home, _____ Get a - long home, _____

Get a-long home, _____ I'll mar-ry you some day.

Bells or recorder

An American Nonsense Song

This song is at least 100 years old. Do you think any popular song of today will be sung 100 years from now?

Clementine

American Folk Song

1. In a cav - ern by a can - yon, Ex - ca - vat - ing for a mine,
2. Light she was and like a feath - er, And her shoes were num - ber nine,

Dwelt a min - er, for - ty - nin - er, And his daugh - ter, Clem-en-tine.
Her - ring box - es with - out top - ses, San - dals were for Clem-en-tine.

Oh, my dar - lin', oh, my dar - lin', Oh, my dar - lin' Clem-en-tine,

You are lost and gone for - ev - er, Dread-ful sor - ry, Clem-en-tine.

3. Drove she ducklings to the water
   Every morning just at nine;
   Struck her foot against a splinter,
   Fell into the foaming brine. *Refrain*

4. Rosy lips above the water
   Blowing bubbles mighty fine;
   But, alas! I was no swimmer,
   So I lost my Clementine. *Refrain*

Add a Harmony Part

Here is the chord pattern for "Clementine." Practice the
chord pattern on the autoharp, then sing the song and play
your own accompaniment.

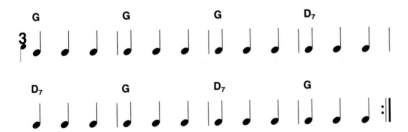

Playing by Ear

You can accompany other songs on the autoharp using the
G and D₇ chords. Try one of these. Start with the G chord
and let your ear tell you when to change from one chord
to the other.

- Skip to My Lou
- Sandy Land
- Frère Jacques
- Polly Wolly Doodle

Singing a Story

Read the words of this song. What kind of story does it tell? A funny story? A sad story?

A song that tells a story is called a *ballad*. How will you use your singing voice to tell the story of the little bug who is looking for a home?

Ballad of the Boll Weevil

Folk Song from the Southern United States

1. The boll wee - vil is a lit - tle black bug,
2. The first time I saw the boll __ weevil,

Come from Mex - i - co, they say, Come all the way to
He was sit - ting on the square. The next time I saw the

Tex - as, Just a - look - ing for a place to stay.
boll weevil, He __ had __ all his fam - 'ly there,

REFRAIN

Just a - look - ing for a home,

Just a - look - ing for a

Just a - look-ing for a home. __

home,

Just a - look - ing for a home.

3. The farmer took the boll weevil
   And he put him in the hot sand.
   The boll weevil said, "This is mighty hot,
   But I'll stand it like a man,
   This'll be my home, . . .

4. The farmer took the boll weevil,
   And he put him on a lump of ice.
   The weevil said to the farmer,
   "This is mighty cool and nice,
   This'll be my home," . . .

5. The merchant got half the cotton,
   The boll weevil got the rest;
   Didn't leave the farmer's wife,
   But one old cotton dress,
   And it's full of holes, . . .

6. The farmer said to his missus,
   "Now what do you think of that?
   The boll weevil has made a nest
   In my best Sunday hat,
   He's got a home, . . .

Pick a Percussion Part

You can use one of these parts to accompany "Ballad of the
Boll Weevil." Which one will you choose?

A Dust Bowl Ballad

Woody Guthrie composed more than 1000 songs that tell about people and their ways of living. Woody called his songs *singing history*.

In this song, Woody tells about the time when most of the Southwest was turned into a "dust bowl."

So Long

Words and Music by Woody Guthrie

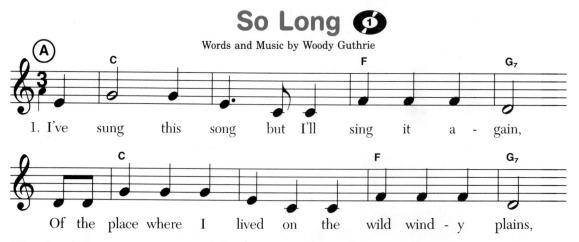

1. I've sung this song but I'll sing it a-gain,

Of the place where I lived on the wild wind-y plains,

In the month called A - pril, the coun - ty called Gray,

And here's what all of the peo - ple there say:

B REFRAIN

"So long, it's been good to know you,

So long, it's been good to know you,

So long, it's been good to know you,

This dust - y old dust is a - get - ting my home,

I've got to be mov - ing a - long." _____

2. A dust storm hit and it hit like thunder,
   It dusted us over and covered us under,
   It blocked out the traffic and blocked out the sun,
   And straight for home all the people did run, singing: *Refrain*

3. We talked of the end of the world, and then
   We'd sing a song, and then sing it again.
   We'd set for an hour and not say a word,
   And then these words would be heard: *Refrain*

Rain Chant

American Indian children take part in the songs and dances of their tribes. At an early age they learn how to beat the drum and shake rattles.

Play a drum beat on your knees as you listen to "Breezes Are Blowing."

Breezes Are Blowing

Luiseño Indian Rain Chant

Breez - es are blow - ing, Blow - ing clouds of wa - ter;

Breez - es are blow - ing, Blow - ing clouds of wa - ter;

On my face, rain - ing, Rain - ing from the o - cean;

Breez - es are blow - ing, Blow - ing clouds of wa - ter.

Add a Part

Drum

Rain rattles

If you play recorder, try playing the melody of "Breezes Are Blowing."

24

 LISTENING SKILLS 1 Listen for rattles and drum in this American Indian music.

Zuni Rain Dance .... **American Indian**

Here is a poem that could be used as part
of a rain-making ceremony.

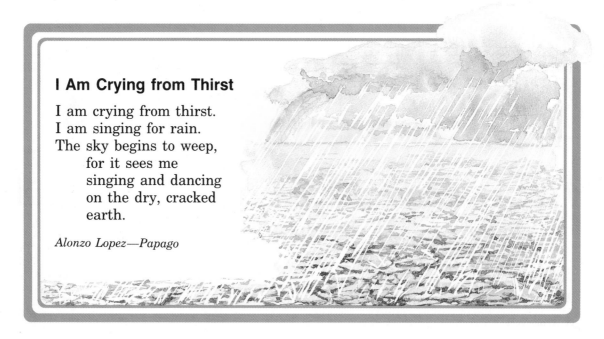

I Am Crying from Thirst

I am crying from thirst.
I am singing for rain.
The sky begins to weep,
    for it sees me
    singing and dancing
    on the dry, cracked
    earth.

Alonzo Lopez—Papago

A Paddling Song

Imagine you are paddling a canoe as you listen to this song. Dip the paddle into the water, then swing it back, ready for the next "dip."

Dip, swing; Dip, swing

Canoe Song

Words and Music by Margaret E. McGhee

I. E MIN   II

1. My pad - dle's keen and bright, Flash - ing with sil - ver.
2. Dip, dip and swing her back, Flash - ing with sil - ver.

III. E MIN   IV

Fol - low the wild goose flight, Dip, dip and swing.
Swift as the wild goose flies, Dip, dip and swing.

When you know the melody of "Canoe Song," sing it as a round with your classmates.

Percussion Parts

Which part will you play to accompany the singing?

Low drum

Rattle

High drum

My pad - dle's keen and bright

Something Told the Wild Geese

Something told the wild geese
  It was time to go.
Though the fields lay golden
  Something whispered—"Snow."
Leaves were green and stirring,
  Berries, luster-glossed,
But beneath warm feathers
  Something cautioned—"Frost."
All the sagging orchards
  Steamed with amber spice,
But each wild breast stiffened
  At remembered ice.
Something told the wild geese
  It was time to fly—
Summer sun was on their wings,
  Winter in their cry.

Rachel Field

A Different Kind of Donkey

The "donkey" these workers are riding is a donkey engine used for loading lumber onto a ship.

Donkey Riding

Canadian Dock-Loaders' Song

1. Were you ev - er in Que - bec, Stow - ing tim - ber
2. Were you ev - er off the Horn, Where it's al - ways

on the deck? Where there's a king with a
fine and warm? Seen _____ the lion and the

gold - en crown, Rid - ing on a don - key.
u - ni - corn, Rid - ing on a don - key.

REFRAIN

Hey, ho! A - way we go! Don - key rid - ing, don - key rid - ing,

Hey, — ho! A - way we go, Rid - ing on a don - key.

3. Were you ever in Cardiff Bay,
   Where the folks all shout "Hooray"?
   Here comes John with his three months' pay,
   Riding on a donkey. *Refrain*

From *Oxford Song Book*, Vol. 2. By permission of Oxford University Press.

A Sailor's Work Song

Shanties were the songs of the men who worked on sailing
ships. The shanteyman sang the solo; the crew answered in
chorus. Listen for the shanteyman's part. It sets the
rhythm for the sailors' work.

Cape Cod Shantey

American Sea Shantey

1. Cape Cod girls, they have no combs, Heave a-way, heave a - way!

They comb their hair with cod-fish bones, We are bound for Aus - tral - ia!

REFRAIN

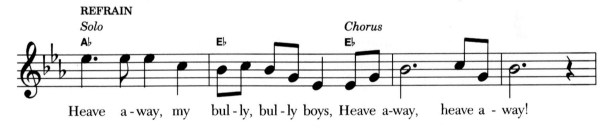

Heave a-way, my bul-ly, bul-ly boys, Heave a-way, heave a - way!

Heave a-way, and don't you make a noise, We are bound for Aus - tral - ia!

2. Cape Cod boys, they have no sleds,
    Heave away, heave away!
   They slide down hill on codfish heads,
    We are bound for Australia! *Refrain*

3. Cape Cod cats, they have no tails,
    Heave away, heave away!
   They blew away in heavy gales,
    We are bound for Australia! *Refrain*

A Song of the Sea

In the old sailing-ship days, whaling crews signed on for voyages that sometimes lasted for three years. The work was hard, and often dangerous. But in the evening, after the day's work was done, the whalers whiled away the time by singing. This is one of the songs they sang.

The Whale

Old Whaling Song

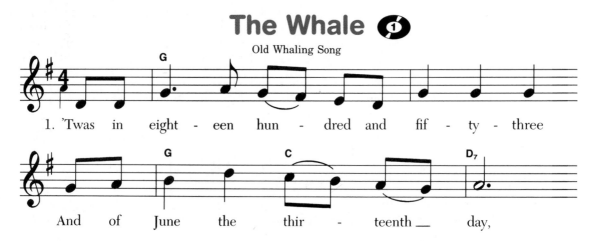

1. 'Twas in eight - een hun - dred and fif - ty - three

And of June the thir - teenth __ day,

That our gal - lant ship her __ an - chor __ weighed,

And for Green - land bore __ a - way, brave boys,

And for Green - land bore __ a - way.

2. The lookout in the crosstrees stood,
   With his spyglass in his hand.
   "There's a whale, there's a whale, there's a whalefish," he cried,
   "And she blows at every span, brave boys,
   And she blows at every span."

3. The captain stood on the quarter-deck,
   And a fine little man was he.
   "Overhaul! Overhaul! Let your davit-tackles fall,
   And launch your boats for sea, brave boys,
   And launch your boats for sea."

4. Now the boats were launched and the men aboard,
   And the whale was in full view;
   Resolv-ed was each seaman bold
   To steer where the whalefish blew, brave boys,
   To steer where the whalefish blew.

5. We struck that whale, the line paid out,
   But she gave a flourish with her tail;
   The boat capsized and four men were drowned,
   And we never caught that whale, brave boys,
   And we never caught that whale.

You will hear a real humpback whale singing at the end of this music.
And God Created Great Whales ...... **Hovhaness**

31

A Quiet Song

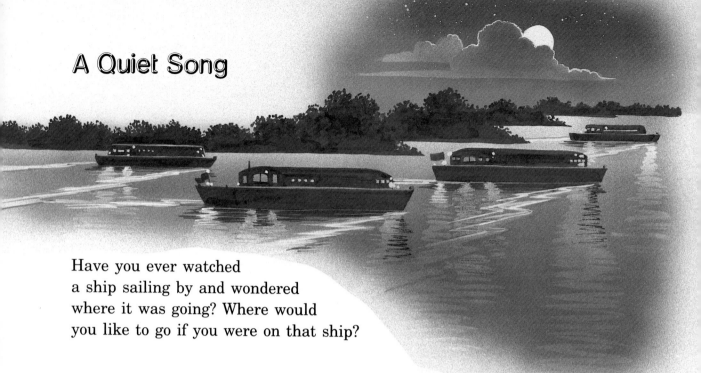

Have you ever watched
a ship sailing by and wondered
where it was going? Where would
you like to go if you were on that ship?

Barges

Traditional

1. Out of my win - dow look - ing in the night,
2. Out of my win - dow look - ing in the night,

I can see the bar - ges' flick' - ring light.
I can see the bar - ges' flick' - ring light.

Si - lent - ly flows the riv - er to the sea,
Star - board shines green and port is glow - ing red,

And the bar - ges, too, go si - lent - ly.
You can see them flick' - ring far a - head.

REFRAIN

Bar - ges, I would like to go with you;

I would like to sail the o - cean blue.

Bar - ges, have you treas - ures in your hold?

Do you fight with pi - rates brave and bold?

Can you find the line that repeats in this poem?

Row the Boat Home

Gently we're gliding over the stream,
   Row, row, row the boat home.
The day's work is over and now we may dream,
   Row, row, row the boat home.

When we rowed up the river, the sunshine was bright,
   Row, row, row the boat home.
And we sang of the morn as we pulled with our might,
   Row, row, row the boat home.

And now falls the evening all gentle and still,
   Row, row, row the boat home.
The shadows are lying on meadow and hill,
   Row, row, row the boat home.

Swiftly we're gliding over the stream,
   Row, row, row the boat home.
The day's work is over, and now we may dream,
   Row, row, row the boat home.

Agnes Lack

33

Railroad Song

Men worked to the rhythm of this old song as they laid the
first railroad tracks in America.

I've Been Working on the Railroad

American Work Song

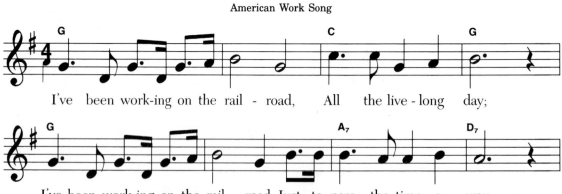

I've been work-ing on the rail - road, All the live - long day;

I've been work-ing on the rail - road, Just to pass the time a - way.

Don't you hear the whis-tle blow - ing?   Rise up so ear-ly in the morn.

Don't you hear the cap-tain shout - ing: "Di - nah, blow your horn!"

Dinah, won't you blow, Dinah, won't you blow,
Dinah, won't you blow your horn?
Dinah, won't you blow, Dinah, won't you blow,
Dinah, won't you blow your horn?

Someone's in the kitchen with Dinah,
Someone's in the kitchen, I know.
Someone's in the kitchen with Dinah,
Strummin' on the old banjo.

Fee, Fie, Fiddle-ee I O,
Fee, Fie, Fiddle-ee I O.
Fee, Fie, Fiddle-ee I O,
Strummin' on the old banjo.

Percussion Parts

Play one of these parts to accompany the singing.

All Aboard!

The title of this song tells you the name of one of the first railroads running west out of Chicago. How many times do you hear the name in the refrain of the song?

Rock Island Line

Railroad Song
New Words and New Arrangement by Huddie Ledbetter
Edited with New Additional Material by Alan Lomax

REFRAIN
I say the Rock Is - land Line is a might-y good road, _

I say the Rock Is - land Line is the road to ride. _

I say the Rock Is - land Line is a might-y good road, _

If you want to ride it, got to ride it like you find it,

Get your tick - et at the sta - tion for the Rock Is - land line.

VERSE

1. May be right and I may be wrong, —
Know you're gon - na miss me ____ when I'm gone.

2. A, B, C, double X, Y, Z,
   Cats in the cupboard, but they don't see me.

The Railroad Cars Are Coming

The great Pacific railway
For California hail!
Bring on the locomotive,
Lay down the iron rail;
Across the rolling prairies,
Through mountain valleys grand,
The railroad cars are coming, humming
Through the prairie land.

The prairie dogs in dog town,
The rattlesnake and quail
Will see the cars a-coming,
Just flying down the rail.
Amid the purple sagebrush,
The antelope will stand
While railroad cars are coming, humming
Through the prairie land.

Traditional

The Music of a Great Locomotive

INSTRUMENTS OF POWER
THOMAS HART BENTON

A Musical Journey

As you listen to the music of *Pacific 231,* follow the locomotive's progress from beginning to end.

Pacific 231 .... Honegger

The following program notes may help you hear some of the things that are going on in the music.

- The great engine is at a standstill, gathering steam.
- The big wheels begin to turn slowly; the locomotive gets underway.
- The locomotive begins to move more quickly, gathering speed.
- The train rushes through the night.
- The great engine slows up.
- The big wheels finally grind to a stop.

38

Train Rhythms

Here are some rhythm patterns that the composer used in *Pacific 231*. The syllables and words under the notes may help you to chant the patterns.

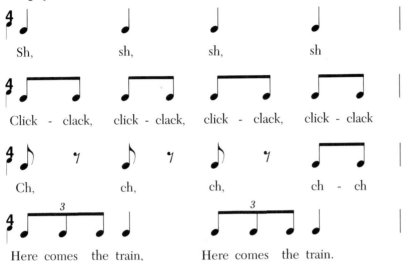

Sh,   sh,   sh,   sh

Click - clack,   click - clack,   click - clack,   click - clack

Ch,   ch,   ch,   ch - ch

Here comes the train,   Here comes the train.

Arthur Honegger
(1892–1953)

The composer Arthur Honegger was born in France in 1892. As a young man he was a fine athlete and was interested in all kinds of sports. Honegger also loved trains and thought of them as roaring giants of power and speed. It is not surprising that he decided to write a piece that would give the feeling of a locomotive. The locomotive that inspired him was an engine of the Pacific type, model number 231. It weighed 300 tons and was designed to pull heavy loads at great speed.

Honegger's composition *Pacific 231* was first performed in Paris, France, in 1923. The performance was a great success, and since that time the piece has been heard in many concert halls throughout the world.

A Solo-Chorus Song

When the recording of "Swing Low, Sweet Chariot" is played, listen for the solo parts; sing along on the chorus parts.

Swing Low, Sweet Chariot

Black Spiritual

3. I'm sometimes up and sometimes down,
   Comin' for to carry me home,
   But still my soul feels heavenly bound,
   Comin' for to carry me home.

Add a Partner Song

Here is another Black Spiritual. It can be sung as a
partner song with the refrain of "Swing Low, Sweet Chariot."

All night, all _____ day, An - gels watch-ing o - ver me my Lord. _____

All night, all _____ day, An - gels watch-ing o - ver me.

Aboard the Glory Train

Follow the words of this song as you listen to the music. Join in on the words *this train* when they come at the end of a line.

This Train 2

Black Spiritual

1. This train is bound for glo - ry, this train, ___

This train is bound for glo - ry, this train, ___

This train is bound for glo - ry, If you ride it you must be ho - ly,

This train is bound for glo - ry, this train. ___

2. This train don't pull no sleepers, this train, . . .
   Don't pull nothin' but the righteous people, . . .

3. This train don't take your money, this train, . . .
   Pay your way with milk and honey, . . .

Collected and adapted by John A. Lomax and Alan Lomax. TRO—© Copyright 1934 and renewed 1962 Ludlow Music, Inc., New York, N.Y. Used by permission.

Play or chant a rhythm accompaniment.

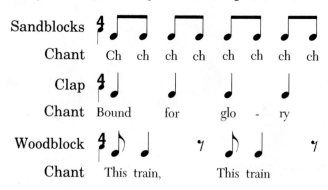

Sandblocks
Chant   Ch ch ch ch ch ch ch ch

Clap
Chant   Bound   for   glo - ry

Woodblock
Chant   This train,   This train

42

Add a Verse

This spiritual tells about two wings, two golden shoes, and
a golden harp. When you know the melody, make up your
own verse for the song.

Two Wings

Black Spiritual

1. Oh, Lord, I want two wings to cov-er ____ my face,
2. I want two gold-en shoes to put on ____ my feet,

Oh, Lord, I want two wings to fly ____ a - way,
I want two gold-en shoes to put on ____ my feet,

Oh, Lord, I want two wings to cov-er ____ my face,
I want two gold-en shoes to put on ____ my feet,

So the world can't do me no harm. ____
So the world can't do me no harm. ____

3. I want a golden harp to play by myself, (3 times)
   So the world can't do me no harm.

Can you find this phrase in the song?

Ab   G   F   Eb

Play the phrase on the bells each time it comes in the song.

43

On the Trail

NIGHT IN OLD WYOMING
FRANK TENNEY JOHNSON

Think about life on the western plains and all the things a cowhand has to do on the job.

I Ride an Old Paint

American Cowboy Song

1. I ride an old paint and I lead an old dan,
2. Oh, when I die take my saddle from the wall,

I'm going to Montana for to throw the hooli-han,
Put it on my pony, lead him out of his stall,

They feed in the coulees and water in the draw,
Tie my bones to his back, turn our faces to the west,

Their tails are all matted and their backs are all raw.
And we'll ride the prairies that we love best.

REFRAIN

Get along, little dogies, get along there slow,

For the fiery and the snuffy are a-rarin' to go.

A Cowhand's Song

This cowhand sings about leaving home and hitting the trail for Mexico.

Old Texas

Oklahoma Cowboy Song

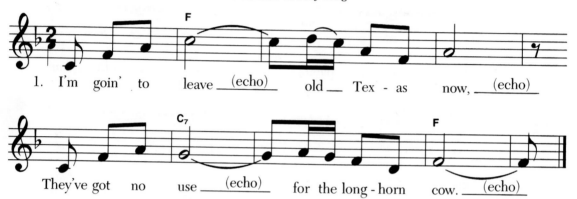

1. I'm goin' to leave ___(echo)___ old ___ Tex - as now, ___(echo)___

They've got no use ___(echo)___ for the long - horn cow. ___(echo)___

2. They've plowed and fenced my cattle range,
   And the people there are all so strange.

3. I'll take my horse, I'll take my rope,
   And hit the trail upon a lope.

4. Say *adios* to the Alamo
   And turn my head toward Mexico.

The melody of "Old Texas" was a favorite in the Old West. Many different sets of words were sung to the same tune. Try putting these words to the "Old Texas" tune.

O bury me not on the lone prairie
Where the coyotes howl and the wind blows free,
Where the buffalo roams o'er a prairie sea,
O bury me not on the lone prairie.

Do you think the man in the poem on page 47 enjoys being a cowboy?

The Cowboy's Life

The bawl of a steer,
To a cowboy's ear,
  Is music of sweetest strain;
And the yelping notes
Of the gay coyotes
  To him are a glad refrain.

For a kingly crown
In the noisy town
  His saddle he wouldn't change;
No life so free
As the life we see
  Way out on the Yaso range.

The rapid beat
Of his broncho's feet
  On the sod as he speeds along,
Keeps living time
To the ringing rhyme
  Of his rollicking cowboy song.

The winds may blow
And the thunder growl
  Or the breezes may safely moan;—
A cowboy's life
Is a royal life,
  His saddle his kingly throne.

John A. Lomax

An Easy-Going Rhythm

Pretend to sway in the saddle as the cowhand's horse lopes easily along the trail.

Git Along, Little Dogies

Cowboy Song

As I was a-walk-ing one morn-ing for pleas-ure,

I spied a cow-punch-er a-rid-ing a-lone;

His hat was thrown back and his spurs was a-jin-gling,

And as he ap-proach'd he was sing-ing this song:

REFRAIN

Whoop-ee ti - yi - yo, git a - long, lit - tle do - gies,

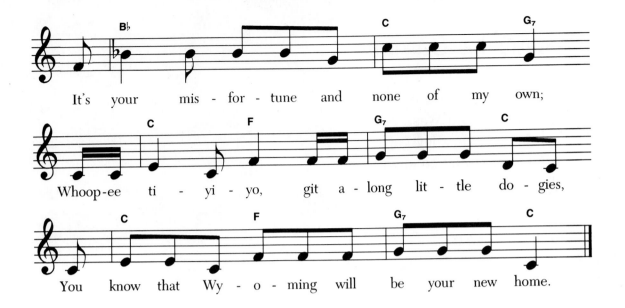

It's your mis - for - tune and none of my own;

Whoop-ee ti - yi - yo, git a - long lit - tle do - gies,

You know that Wy - o - ming will be your new home.

2. It's early in spring that we round up the dogies,
   We mark them and brand them and bob off their tails;
   We round up our horses, load up the chuck wagon,
   And then throw the dogies out onto the trail.
   Refrain

3. It's whooping and yelling and driving the dogies,
   And oh, how I wish you would only go on;
   It's whooping and punching, go on, little dogies,
   You know that Wyoming will be your new home.
   Refrain

Percussion Accompaniments

Add one of these rhythms to accompany the singing.
Autoharp players can follow the chord letters in the music.

Around the Campfire

Cowpunchers like to talk about the days of the Old West. After a hard day's work, they gather around the campfire to sing and to tell tall tales. Here is one of the tall tales they like best.

Great Granddad

American Cowboy Song

1. Great Grand - dad, when the land was young,
Barred the door with a wag - on tongue,
For the times was rough and the dan - gers great,
And he said his prayers both ear - ly and late.

2. He was a citizen tough and grim,
Danger was duck soup to him,
He ate corn pone and bacon fat,
Said his great grandson would starve on that.

3. Twenty-one children came to bless
The old man's house in the wilderness,
They slept on the floor with the dogs and cats,
And they hunted in the woods in their coonskin hats.

From THE COWBOY SINGS edited by Kenneth S. Clark. Copyright 1932, Shawnee Press, Inc., Delaware Water Gap, PA 18327. Used by permission.

A Cowboy from Brooklyn

Aaron Copland has written a lot of music about America.
In some of his pieces he used real cowboy songs to make
the music sound more western.

For his one-act ballet *Billy the Kid,* Copland borrowed two
of the cowboy tunes that are printed in your book—"Great
Granddad" and "Git Along, Little Dogies." Can you hear
them in this recording?

"Street in a Frontier Town"
from *Billy the Kid* ....Copland

Songs of the Vendors

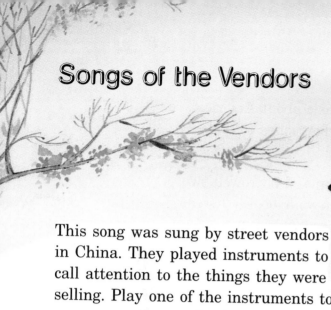

This song was sung by street vendors in China. They played instruments to call attention to the things they were selling. Play one of the instruments to accompany the vendors' songs.

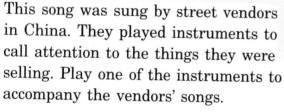

Feng Yang Song

Folk Song from China

1. Sing the Feng Yang Song; Sing it loud and long. Clash cym - bals,
2. Gifts for you have I, Kites that swoop and fly; Small trin - kets,

beat the drum, Strike the met - al gong! We are the ven - dors who
man - y toys, All of you may buy. Pa - per of gold shin - ing,

trav - el all day long, Call - ing our wares to the Feng_ Yang_ Song.
Bam - boo smooth and strong, Call - ing the clear, ring - ing toy - man's_ song.

REFRAIN

Feng yang, fong yong, beat the gong, __ Strike the clap - pers well.

Clash cym-bals, byah yah yang, Clash cym-bals, byah yah yang! Brr dong!

Brr dong! Brr dong yah feng yang, fang yong, Brr, beat the drum!

3. Shave I have for you,
   Smooth—neat and true.
   Trimming and cutting hair,
   All of that I do.
   Keenness and skill
   To my instruments belong,
   Calling the clear, ringing
   Barber's song. *Refrain*

4. Fortune's magic spell
   I know very well;
   Dry sticks of ancient wood
   Always good foretell.
   Come, try your luck
   For the sticks are never wrong,
   Call the clear, ringing
   Fortune teller's song. *Refrain*

Here is an old street cry that was sung in another part of
the world—England. It might have been the cry of one
vendor. Or three different vendors might have been selling
their wares at the same time. Try singing their cries as a round.

Chairs to Mend

Traditional

Chairs to mend, old chairs to mend.

Mack - er - el, fresh mack - er - el.

Rags, rags, an - y old rags?

An Old English Ballad

Follow the words of this ballad as you listen to the song. Then tell the story of the lady and the gypsies in your own words.

The Wraggle-Taggle Gypsies

Old English Ballad

1. There _ were three gyp - sies a - come to my door,
2. Then _ she pulled off her _ silk fin - ished gown,

And down - stairs ran this _ la - dy, O!
And put on hose of _ leath - er, O!

The first sang high and the sec - ond sang low,
The rag - ged rags a - bout _ our door,

And the third sang "Bon - ny, bon - ny Bis - cay, O!"
And she's gone with the wrag - gle - tag - gle gyp - sies, O!

54

3. It was late last night when my lord came home,
   Inquiring for his lady, O!
   The servants said on ev'ry hand,
   "She's gone with the wraggle-taggle gypsies, O!"

4. "Come, saddle to me my milk-white steed,
   And go and seek my pony, O!
   That I may ride and seek my bride,
   Who is gone with the wraggle-taggle gypsies, O!"

5. Then he rode high, and he rode low,
   He rode through wood and copses too.
   Until he came to an open field,
   And there he espied his a-lady, O!

6. "What makes you leave your house and land?
   What makes you leave your money, O?
   What makes you leave your new-wedded lord,
   To go with the wraggle-taggle gypsies, O?"

7. "What care I for my house and land?
   And what care I for my money, O?
   What care I for my new-wedded lord?
   I'm off with the wraggle-taggle gypsies, O!"

8. "Last night you slept in a goose-feather bed
   With the sheet turned down so bravely, O!
   But tonight you sleep in a cold, open field,
   Along with the wraggle-taggle gypsies, O!"

9. "Oh, what care I for a goose-feather bed
   With the sheet turned down so bravely, O!
   For tonight I shall sleep in a cold, open field,
   Along with the wraggle-taggle gypsies, O!"

A Ballad from Down Under

In Australia, men going from one job to another carry all their possessions in a blanket roll—a Matilda.

Follow the words of the song as you listen to the music. What finally happened to the swagman?

Waltzing Matilda ②

Words by A. B. Patterson   Music by Maria Cowan

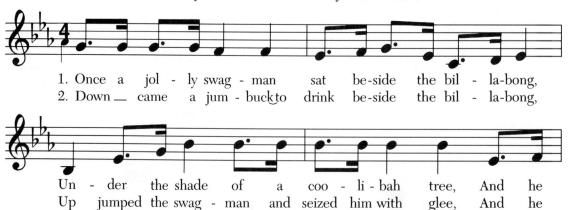

1. Once a jol - ly swag - man sat be - side the bil - la - bong,
2. Down — came a jum - buck to drink be - side the bil - la - bong,

Un - der the shade of a coo - li - bah tree, And he
Up jumped the swag - man and seized him with glee, And he

sang   as   he sat   and   wait - ed till   his bil - ly boiled,
sang   as   he talked to that   jum - buck in   his tuck - er - bag,

"You'll   come   a - waltz - ing,   Ma - til - da,   with me."
"You'll   come   a - waltz - ing,   Ma - til - da,   with me."

REFRAIN

Waltz - ing   Ma - til - da,   waltz - ing   Ma - til - da,
Waltz - ing   Ma - til - da,   waltz - ing   Ma - til - da,

You'll   come   a - waltz - ing   Ma - til - da,   with me.   And   he
You'll   come   a - waltz - ing   Ma - til - da,   with me.   And   he

sang   as   he sat   and   wait - ed till   his bil - ly boiled
sang   as   he talked to that   jum - buck in   his tuck - er - bag,

"You'll   come   a - waltz - ing,   Ma - til - da,   with me."
"You'll   come   a - waltz - ing,   Ma - til - da,   with me."

3. Down came the stockman, riding on his thoroughbred,
   Down came the troopers, one, two, three.
   "Where's the jolly jumbuck you've got in your tuckerbag?
   You'll come a-waltzing, Matilda, with me." *Refrain*

4. Up jumped the swagman and plunged into the billabong,
   "You'll never catch me alive," cried he;
   And his ghost may be heard as you ride beside the billabong,
   "You'll come a-waltzing, Matilda, with me." *Refrain*

A Bird that Laughs

The kookaburra is a bird found in Australia. Its call
sounds like loud laughter.

Kookaburra

Words and Music by Marion Sinclair

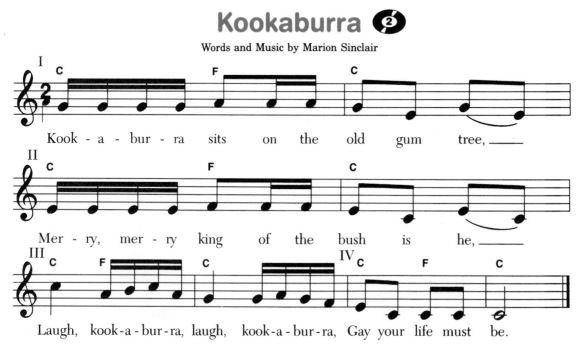

Kook - a - bur - ra sits on the old gum tree, _____

Mer - ry, mer - ry king of the bush is he, _____

Laugh, kook - a - bur - ra, laugh, kook - a - bur - ra, Gay your life must be.

Organize an orchestra for "Kookaburra." Will you play a rhythm pattern on a percussion instrument, a melody pattern on the bells, or will you strum an accompaniment pattern on the autoharp?

Percussion Patterns

Can you find these patterns in the song?

Bell Patterns

Autoharp Pattern

Follow the chord names in the music as you strum this steady-beat pattern.

A Calypso Song

In the West Indies, calypso singers travel from place to place singing in each village they visit. Their songs are often made up on the spot and tell about people and news events of the day. This calypso song tells about Miss Mary Ann.

Mary Ann

West Indian Calypso

1. All day, all night, Miss Ma-ry Ann,_____

Down by the sea - shore sift - ing sand._____

Ev - en lit - tle chil - dren join in the band_____

Down by the sea - shore sift - ing sand._____

2. All day, all night, Miss Mary Ann,
   Down by the seashore sifting sand,
   Young and old come join the band
   Down by the seashore sifting sand.

3. All day, all night, Miss Mary Ann,
   Down by the seashore sifting sand,
   Everybody come and join the band
   Down by the seashore sifting sand.

Be a calypso singer and make up a new verse about Mary Ann.

Percussion Parts

You can accompany "Mary Ann" on one of the percussion instruments pictured in your book. Which pattern will you choose?

Buenos Dias

"La Cucaracha" is one of the most popular Mexican folk songs. If you know the melody, sing along with the recording.

La Cucaracha

Folk Melody from Mexico   Words by Richard Eisman

1. There's a bug, some like to chase it,   When we play we must out-race it,

If at lunch we see it com - ing,   We're sup-posed to send it run - ning.

REFRAIN

La cu - ca - ra - cha, la cu - ca - ra - cha,   I'm so sad to see you go.

La cu - ca - ra - cha, la cu - ca - ra - cha,   I love you; *te quie-ro   yo.*

2. Tiny thing with no *amigos,*
   Not a friend wherever it goes,
   Do you really want to banish
   Little bugs who sing in Spanish?

3. Let the bugs enjoy their freedom,
   Even though we do not need 'em,
   All *las niñas* and *los niños*
   Can't forget their true *amigos.*

Here are the Spanish words of "La Cucaracha." Try to follow them as you listen to the recording. You might want to try singing along.

1. *Una cucaracha pinta,*
   Le dijo a una colorada,
   Vámonos para mi tierra,
   A pasar la temporada.

Refrain
   La cucaracha, la cucaracha,
   Ya no quiere caminar,
   Porque no tiena, porque le falta,
   Dinero para gastar.

2. *Todas las muchachas tienen,*
   En los ojos dos estrellas,
   Pero las mexicanitas,
   De seguro son más bellas. (Refrain)

3. *Una cosa me da risa,*
   Pancho Villa sin camisa;
   Ya se van los carrancistas,
   Porque vienen los villistas. (Refrain)

Here is another popular Mexican song, performed by a mariachi ensemble. Listen for the trumpets, violins, and guitars.

Cielito lindo .... **Mexican Folk Song**

South African Plains Song

Show that you hear the two sections in this song by doing a different hand pattern for each section.

In section A, pat knees and clap hands.

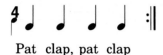

Pat clap, pat clap

In section B, snap fingers and clap hands.

Snap clap, snap clap
right   left

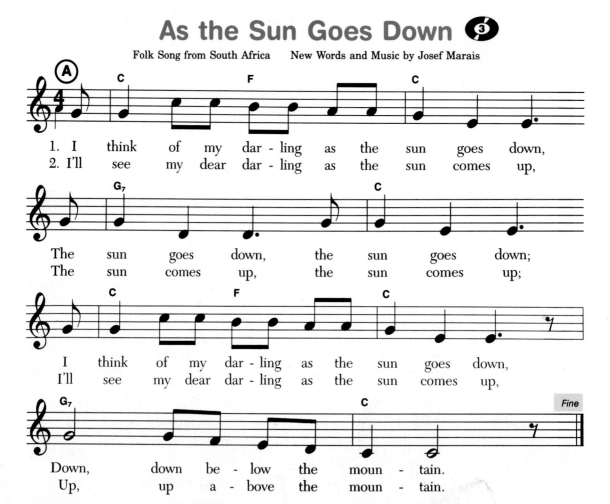

As the Sun Goes Down

Folk Song from South Africa   New Words and Music by Josef Marais

1. I think of my dar - ling as the sun goes down,
2. I'll see my dear dar - ling as the sun comes up,

The sun goes down, the sun goes down;
The sun comes up, the sun comes up;

I think of my dar - ling as the sun goes down,
I'll see my dear dar - ling as the sun comes up,

Down, down be - low the moun - tain.
Up, up a - bove the moun - tain.

B F   C

I'll ride, I'll ride, I'll ride, I'll ride, I'll ride all night,

G₇   C

when the moon is bright, when the moon is bright;

F

I'll ride, I'll ride, I'll ride, I'll ride, I'll

C   D₇   G₇   D.C. al Fine

ride all night; I'll get there in the morn - ing.

A Countermelody for Section B

I'll ride all night, Ride all night,

Ride all night I'll get there in the morn - ing

A Nonsense Song

Rag Mop

Words and Music by Johnnie Lee Wills and Deacon Anderson

1. M, I say M - O, M - O - P, M - O - P - P, _____ Mop!
   M - O - P - P, Mop! Mop! Mop! Mop! Rag Mop! Rag Mop! Rag Mop! Rag Mop! R - A - G - G, M - O - P - P, Rag Mop!

2. R, I say R - A, R - A - G, R - A - G - G, _____ Rag!
   R - A - G - G, M - O - P - P. Rag Mop!

3. A, I say A - B, A - B - C, A - B - C - D, _____ A - B - C - D - E, A - B - C - D - E - F - G - H.

4. M, I say M-O, M-O-P, M-O-P-P, Mop!
   M-O-P-P, Mop, Mop, Mop, Mop! *Refrain*

5. R, I say R-A, R-A-G,
   R-A-G-G, RAG! R-A-G-G, M-O-P-P
   Refrain

Pattern for Four Players

You will need four players and four different percussion instruments to play this accompaniment for "Rag Mop."

Play when the picture of your instrument is shown under the note. Feel the beat and keep the pattern going all through the song.

Rock an' Roll

Like all rock songs, this popular song of the 1950s has a strong, steady beat. Find a way to show the steady beat as you listen to the music. The headline at the top of the page may give you an idea.

At the Hop

Words and Music by Arthur Singer, John Medora, and David White

1. Well you can rock it, you can roll it, do the stomp and e-ven stroll it at the hop.
2. Well you can swing it, you can groove it, you can real-ly start to move it at the hop.

When the rec-ord starts a-spin-nin' you ca-lyp-so when you chick-en at the hop.
Where the jump-in' is the smooth-est and the mu-sic is the cool-est at the hop.

Do the dance sen-sa-tion that is sweep-in' the na-tion at the hop.
All the cats and chicks __ will go to get __ their kicks _____ at the hop.

Let's go to the hop! ___ Let's go to the hop! ___

Let's go to the hop! ___ Let's go to the hop! ___

Ah, Ah, Let's go to the hop! ___

Do you find this pattern in section A or in section B? How many times do you find it?

Try playing the pattern every time it comes in the song. You will need these bells.

Dance Music: Old and New

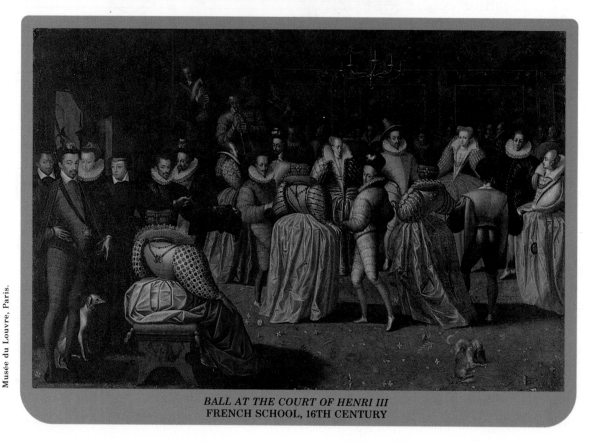

BALL AT THE COURT OF HENRI III
FRENCH SCHOOL, 16TH CENTURY

People have enjoyed dancing for hundreds and hundreds of years. In olden times people danced at the court—in palaces of kings and queens. Other people danced to folk music in the open air on village greens. Later on, people danced in ballrooms and on theater stages all over the world. Where do people dance today? What kind of dances do they do?

You will hear two dances. One is very old—from the 16th century. The other was written 400 years later, in the 20th century. Listen for three things: melody, rhythm, and instruments.

"Bergerette" .... **Anonymous**
"Devil's Dance" from
The Soldier's Tale .... **Stravinsky**

What makes the two pieces different?

70

As you listen to "Bergerette" again, try following the melody. Which section is repeated—A or B?

Igor Stravinsky was born in Russia in 1882. His father was a famous singer at the Russian Imperial Opera. Stravinsky often went to opera rehearsals and ballet performances with his father and learned to love the musical theater when he was still a young boy.

Stravinsky intended to become a lawyer but by the time he was twenty one, he knew he wanted to be a composer. During his lifetime, Stravinsky composed many pieces for the musical theater, including the short ballet, *The Soldier's Tale*. "Devil's Dance" is one of the pieces from *The Soldier's Tale*.

Igor Stravinsky
(1882–1971)

Test 1 ✔

Look in the right-hand column for the exact echo of the music in the left-hand column. On your worksheet, write its letter in the blank.

1. _____

A

2. _____

B

3. _____

C

4. _____

D

5. _____

E

In the song "I Love Music," some of the short phrases are followed by a part that is an exact repetition. On this recording, you will hear six musical examples. Each example has two phrases. If the second phrase is exactly like the first phrase, circle the word EXACT on your worksheet. If the second phrase is not exactly like the first phrase, circle the words NOT EXACT.

1.   EXACT   NOT EXACT

2.   EXACT   NOT EXACT

3.   EXACT   NOT EXACT

4.   EXACT   NOT EXACT

5.   EXACT   NOT EXACT

6.   EXACT   NOT EXACT

What Do You Hear 2

1. You will hear three songs. Choose the person who would most likely be singing each song. Would it be a cowhand, a railroad worker, or a sailor? On your worksheet, circle your answer for each example.

a. cowhand	railroad worker	sailor
b. cowhand	railroad worker	sailor
c. cowhand	railroad worker	sailor

2. You will hear three pieces. Choose the place where each piece might be heard. Would you hear it on a city street, in a church, or at a dance? On your worksheet, circle your answer for each example.

a. city street	church	dance
b. city street	church	dance
c. city street	church	dance

Test 2 ✓

On your worksheet, write the letter of the correct answer
in the blank.

1. A composer whose songs are so well-known that they

   are called *folk songs* is _____.
   (a) Igor Stravinsky   (b) Stephen Foster   (c) Arthur Honegger

2. Work songs are songs people sing to help them do a

   hard job. An example of such a song is _____.
   (a) "Getting to Know You" (b) "Leatherwing Bat" (c) "Donkey Riding"

3. "Swing Low, Sweet Chariot," "This Train," and "Two

   Wings" are all _____.
   (a) shanties   (b) Black Spirituals   (c) songs of transportation

4. Work songs sung by sailors are called _____.
   (a) shanties   (b) Black Spirituals   (c) calypso songs

5. Among the many groups of workers who have

   contributed to our folk music are _____.
   (a) cowpunchers   (b) dancers   (c) kookaburras

6. One of the songs that Woody Guthrie wrote about the

   "dust bowl" in the Southwest is _____.
   (a) "Clementine"   (b) "Ballad of the Boll Weevil"   (c) "So Long"

7. The *matilda* in the song "Waltzing Matilda" is a _____.
   (a) rabbit   (b) frying pan   (c) blanket roll

8. Many folk songs have a part that is repeated in the

   same way after each verse. It is called _____.
   (a) repeat   (b) refrain   (c) finale

9. What are people doing at the "hop"? _____
   (a) skating   (b) working   (c) dancing

10. Songs sung by vendors are called _____.
    (a) ballads   (b) street cries   (c) solo-chorus songs

Tone Color

Melody

Rhythm

UNDERSTANDING MUSIC

Harmony

A B C Form

Steady Beat

Here is a story about a man named Joe. Follow the words as you listen to the recording.

Hi! My Name Is Joe, Version 1

Hi! My name is Joe. I've got a wife and three kids. I work in a button factory.

One day my boss came to me and said, "Joe, are you busy?" I said, "No." He said, "Turn the button with your right hand. Turn the button with your left hand. Turn the button with your right foot. Turn the button with your left foot. Turn the button with your right elbow. Turn the button with your left elbow. Turn the button with your head. Joe, are you busy?" I said, "Yes!"

Now follow the words at the top of the next page as you listen to another version of Joe's story. Can you discover how this version is different?

Hi! My Name is Joe, **Version 2**

Hi! My name is Joe. I've got-ta

wife and three kids. I work in a but-ton fac-to-

ry. One day my boss came to me and said,

"Joe, are you bus-y?" I said, "No."

He said, "Turn the but-ton with your right hand."

Chant a Rhyme

Play a steady beat on a percussion instrument as you chant one of these rhymes.

- A diller, a dollar, a ten o'clock scholar.
  What makes you come so soon?
  You used to come at ten o'clock
  But now you come at noon.

- The Man in the Moon as he sails the sky
  Is a very remarkable skipper.
  But he made a mistake when he tried to take
  A drink of milk from the dipper.
  He dipped right into the Milky Way
  And slowly and carefully filled it.
  The Big Bear growled and the Little Bear howled,
  And frightened him so he spilled it.

Sets of Two–Meter in 2

Tap the steady beat on your lap as you listen to this song about camping.

Going Camping 3

Words and Music by Ray Charles

F

I got my gear in my pack, I got my

F

pack on my back, To - day's the day I'm go - ing

C7

camp - ing; Just got the go - a - head sign, The weath-er's

gon - na be fine, To - day's the day I'm go - ing

camp - ing. I'm gon - na pitch me a tent, won't have to

pay an - y rent, It looks like ev - 'ry - thing is A - O -

K; As far as I can see I think it's

gon - na be a per - fect camp - ing day. ____

Play a Part

Practice one of the parts from this arrangement for percussion instruments. When you are ready, play it as an accompaniment for "Going Camping."

Guiro — Play throughout

Woodblock — Play throughout

Triangle — Play throughout

Drum — Play throughout

Sets of Three—Meter in 3

Tap the steady beat on your lap as you listen to this folk song from Austria.

Cuckoo

English Words by Katherine F. Rohrbough   Folk Song from Austria

1. Oh, I went to the flow - ing spring where the wa - ter's so good; And I heard there the cuck - oo as she called from the wood.
2. Af - ter Eas - ter come sun - ny days that will melt all the snow; Then I'll mar - ry my maid - en fair, we'll be hap - py I know.
3. When I've mar - ried my maid - en fair what then can I de - sire? Oh, a home for our tend - ing and some wood for the fire.

REFRAIN

Hoh - lee - ah, Hoh - leh - rah - hee - hee - ah,

Hoh - leh - rah cuck - oo. Hoh - leh - rah - hee - hee - ah,

Hoh - leh - rah cuck - oo. Hoh - leh - rah - hee - hee - ah,

Hoh - leh - rah cuck - oo, Hoh - leh-rah - hee - hee - ah - hoh.

Play a Part

To help you feel the beats moving in sets of three, choose one
of these parts to play with "Cuckoo."

SECTION A

Autoharp strum

Bell Part 1

Bell Part 2

SECTION B

Tambourine

Woodblock

Twos or Threes

Each verse of this Irish song tells more and more about the "tree in the bog."

As you listen to the music, decide how the beats are grouped. Are they grouped in sets of two or in sets of three?

The Rattlin' Bog

Folk Song from Ireland

REFRAIN

Oh, row, the rat - tlin' bog, The bog down in the val - ley, oh,

Oh, row, the rat - tlin' bog, The bog down in the val - ley, oh.

VERSE

1. And in that bog there was a tree,
2. And on that tree there was a bough,

A rare tree, and a rat - tlin' tree,
bough, bough,

(1.) And the tree in the bog, And the tree in the bog,
(2.) And the bough on the tree, And the tree in the bog,

And the bog down in the val - ley, oh.

3. Now on that bough there was a branch,
   A rare branch, and a rattlin' branch,
   And the branch on the bough,
   And the bough on the tree,
   And the tree in the bog,
   And the bog down in the valley, oh. *Refrain*

4. Now on that branch there was a nest,
   A rare nest, and a rattlin' nest,
   And the nest on the branch,
   And the branch on the bough,
   And the bough on the tree,
   And the tree in the bog,
   And the bog down in the valley, oh. *Refrain*

5. Now in that nest there was a bird,
   A rare bird, and a rattlin' bird,
   And the bird in the nest,
   And the nest on the branch . . . *Refrain*

6. And on that bird there was a tail . . . *Refrain*

Play a Part

These percussion parts can be used to accompany the refrain of "The Rattlin' Bog." Which part will you play?

Twos or Threes?

As you listen to this song, decide how the beats are grouped. Are they grouped in sets of two or in sets of three? Try doing one of these hand patterns in time to the music.

PAT-clap-clap, PAT-clap-clap
CLAP-snap-snap, CLAP-snap-snap

The Dreamer

Words by Alfred Kreymborg   Music by Elie Siegmeister

1. I love all the clouds that go sail - ing a - way,

And I'd love to be one of the ships for a day

In a sea that is blue as the sky is to - day,

is to - day.

2. I'd love to go fishing beside an old stream,
   And wishing no more than I wish in a dream,
   To catch just the sun at the end of a beam,
      of a beam.

3. I'd love to go riding the wind or a breeze,
   And ripple the stream or pass over the seas,
   And land on an island, the island of peace,
      of peace.

4. I'd love to come home with the stars in the night,
   And give ev'ry fellow a little more light,
   And hold out my hand to him, then say "goodnight,
      goodnight."

Steady Beat—Strong Beat

The number in the color box in each pattern below tells you
how many beats there are in each measure.

Play the STEADY beat softly on a low drum.

Play the STRONG beat on finger cymbals.

Royal Fireworks

LORD MAYOR'S DAY PROCESSION BY WATER
PATON & WHEATLEY

George Frideric Handel composed *Royal Fireworks Music* for an outdoor spectacle including fireworks and a one hundred and one cannon salute.

You will hear two pieces from *Royal Fireworks Music*. The title of each piece is the name of an old dance. "Bourrée" is in 2 meter; "Minuet" is in 3 meter.

"Bourrée" from *Royal Fireworks Music* ... Handel
"Minuet" from *Royal Fireworks Music* .... Handel

Here is the first theme of "Bourrée." What sign in the music tells you the piece is in 2 meter?

Here is the first theme of "Minuet." What sign in the music tells you the piece is in 3 meter?

George Frideric Handel
1685–1759

George Frideric Handel was born in the small German city of Halle in 1685. When he was still a child, Handel decided that he would be a musician when he grew up. But his father had other plans—he wanted his son to become a lawyer.

At first, Handel's father (who didn't think much of music) ordered George to give up the silly notion of becoming a musician. But later on he recognized his son's musical gifts and arranged for George to have the finest music teachers.

During his lifetime, Handel spent a lot of time travelling from one country to another. He finally settled in England where he composed many pieces, including *Royal Fireworks Music,* that are still favorites with concert audiences all over the world.

The Sounds Around Us

The world is full of sounds—long sounds, short sounds. Listen to the sounds around you right now. What do you hear?

How many long sounds can you make with your voice? How many short sounds? Experiment.

Find ways to make long and short sounds on instruments in your classroom. Try one of these: autoharp, tambourine, woodblock, sandblocks, triangle, drum.

You might use long and short sounds when you chant at a high school football game.

We want a touch-down! We want a touch-down!

Block that kick! Block that kick!

Notice the long and short sounds in this chant.

Base-ball base-ball, Let's play base-ball.

Bat-ter up, bat-ter up, Let's play ball!

There are long and short sounds in music, too. Listen for long and short sounds in your favorite song.

Long/Short Sounds

Can you hear long and short sounds in this piece for
piano? As each number is called on the recording, look at
the chart. It will help you hear long and short sounds as
the music goes along.

1. LONG SOUNDS ▬▬▬ ▬▬ ▬▬ ▬▬▬

2. SHORT SOUNDS ▬ ▬ ▬ ▬ ▬ ▬ ▬

3. LONG SOUNDS ▬▬ ▬▬ ▬▬ ▬▬▬

4. SHORT SOUNDS ▬ ▬ ▬ ▬ ▬ ▬ ▬

5. SHORT SOUNDS ▬ ▬ ▬ ▬ ▬ ▬ ▬

6. LONG SOUNDS ▬▬▬ ▬▬ ▬▬ ▬▬▬

7. LONG SOUNDS ▬▬▬ ▬▬ ▬▬ ▬▬▬

When you listen to this music on another day, try to hear
the long and short sounds without looking at the chart.

Long and Short Sounds in a Song

Listen for long and short sounds in this song.

At the Spring
(Koni au i ka wai)

Song from Hawaii   Words and Music by King Kalakaua   English Words by Liliana Wahine

Of the cool wa - ters fresh at the spring,
Ko - ni au ko - ni au i ka wai,

Of their cool won - der now let us sing;
Ko - ni au i ka wai hu - i hui;

Of the gift of health that they give to all,
I ka wai a - lii a - ke ki - ni la,

And the pleas - ure to us the wa - ters bring.
O - lu ai ka - no - ho - na o ka lai.

Long and short sounds can be combined to make a rhythm pattern. Follow the rhythm pattern of each line of the song as you listen to the music.

COLOR PLANES IN OVAL
PIET MONDRIAN

Listening for Long and Short Sounds

Listen for the patterns of long and short sounds in "Polka Melody."

 "Polka Melody"

As you listen to "Polka Melody" again, follow the rhythm pattern in each line of the music printed below. In which lines do you hear the longest sound?

A composer from Bohemia used the "Polka Melody" tune in a comic opera called *Schwanda the Bagpiper.* According to an old legend, Schwanda was no ordinary bagpipe player. He was more like a "pied piper" who chased away all troubles with his merry tunes.

 Listen how the melody is used in this piece for orchestra.
"Polka" from *Schwanda the Bagpiper* .. Weinberger

94

Two Different Patterns

You will hear two versions of this old English round. Can you
tell how they are alike? How they are different?

For Health and Strength

Old English Round

Version 1

For health and strength and dai - ly food We praise Thy name, O Lord.

Version 2

For health and strength and dai - ly food We praise Thy name, O Lord.

When you know the melody of "For Health and Strength,"
your class can sing the song as a two-part round. Try
version 1 first, then try version 2.

Percussion Patterns

Try playing these patterns on a percussion instrument. Choose
a different-sounding instrument for each pattern.

Careers in Music

The photographs on these two pages show David McHugh in a variety of roles—family man, composer, singer, pianist. On the recording, Mr. McHugh talks about his career in music.

 Careers in Music—David McHugh

Music and Rain

DOWNPOUR
ZOLTAN SZABO

Notice how the composer uses repeated tones in this melody.

Rain Song

Words and Music by David McHugh

The rain just keeps on fall - ing, And the sky is col-ored grey;

The birds don't stop their sing-ing — 'Cause it's just an-oth-er day;

And the clouds keep pass-ing o - ver, Bring-in' rain to flow'rs be - low;

While the sun keeps wait-ing pa-tient-ly To un-veil its gold-en glow;

Some-times sun shines, and oth-er times it rains; _____

But to me it's all the same, _____

To me it's all the same. _____

LISTENING SKILLS 4 Listen for repeated tones in a piano piece by Frèdèric Chopin.
"Raindrop" Prelude .... **Chopin**

Spring Rain

Leaves make a slow
Whispering sound
As the drops go
Drip to the ground
    Peace, peace, says the tree.

Good wet rain!
Shout happy frogs,
Peepers and big green
Bulls in bogs,
    Lucky, lucky are we!

On a bough above,
Head under wing,
A mourning dove
Waits time to sing.
    Ah me, she sighs, ah me! *Harry Behn*

How Tones Move

Look at the notes in the color boxes.
In which direction do they move?

My Favorite Things 4
(from The Sound of Music)

Words by Oscar Hammerstein II   Music by Richard Rodgers

Rain - drops on   ros - es   and   whisk - ers on   kit - tens,
Cream col - ored   pon - ies   and   crisp ap - ple   strud - els,

Bright cop - per   ket - tles   and   warm wool - en   mit - tens,
Door - bells and   sleigh - bells and   schnitz - el with   noo - dles,

Brown pa - per   pack - ag - es   tied   up   with   strings,
Wild geese that   fly   with   the   moon   on   their   wings,

These   are   a   few   of   my   fa - vor - ite   things.
These   are   a   few   of   my   fa - vor - ite   things.

Girls in white dress - es with blue sat - in sash - es,

Snow - flakes that stay on my nose and eye - lash - es,

Sil - ver white win - ters that melt in - to springs,

These are a few of my fa - vor - ite things.

When the dog bites, when the bee stings,

when I'm feel - ing sad, _____ I

sim - ply re - mem - ber my fa - vor - ite things and

then I don't feel _____ so

bad. _____

A Tall Tale

This song tells the story of a man with a very long name.
As you listen to the music, join in on the refrain when you can.

Sama Kama Wacky Brown

Words and Music by George Goehring and Edward Warn

Ed - die coo chee catch-ee kam - a tos a near - a tos a nok - a

sam - a kam - a wack-y ___ Brown, ___ Fell in-to the well,

Fell in-to the well, ___ Fell in-to the deep dark well.

1. Su - sie Jones, milk - in' in the barn,
2. Su - sie's ma, bak - in' crack - lin' bread,
3. Then Old John put his plow a - side,
4. To the well, Ev - 'ry bod - y came,

To Coda last time D.C.

Saw him fall, ran in - side and told her ma that
Called Old John, told him that her Su - sie said that
Grabbed his cane, hob - bled in - to town and cried that
What a shame! It took so long to say his name that

Coda

Ed - die coo chee catch - ee kam - a tos a near - a tos a nok - a

[1.]
sam - a kam - a wack - y _____ Brown, _____

[2.]
sam - a kam - a wack - y _____ Brown, _____ drowned!

Find the notes in the color box. In which direction do they move?

Bell Part for Refrain

How do the tones move in this bell part?

Up and Down the Road

Follow the yellow brick road!

We're Off to See the Wizard 4
(from the Wonderful Wizard of Oz)

Words by E. Y. Harburg   Music by Harold Arlen

Fol-low the yel-low brick road, — Fol-low the yel-low brick road, —

Fol - low, fol - low, fol - low, fol - low, fol-low the yel-low brick road. —

Fol - low   the   rain - bow   o - ver   the   stream,

Fol - low   the   fel - low   who   fol - lows   a   dream.

Fol - low, fol - low, fol - low, fol - low, Fol-low the yel-low brick road.

104

A Yodeling Song

In this song, Swiss hikers yodel across the valley to their friends. Listen for the yodels in the recording.

Weggis Song

Swiss Folk Song

1. From Lu-cerne to — Weg-gis fair,
2. On the lake we — all shall row, Hol-di-ri-di-a, hol-di-ri-a,
3. Weg-gis hills are — not so far,

Shoes and stock-ings we need not wear,
Look-ing at the — fish be-low, Hol-di-ri-di-a, hol-di-a.
We will all out — "Hei-sa-sa,"

REFRAIN

Hol - di - ri - di - a, hol - di - ri - di - a, hol - di - ri - a,

Hol - di - ri - di - a, hol - di - ri - di - a, hol - di - a.

Steps, Leaps, Repeats

Can you hear steps, leaps, and repeats in a melody?

As each number is called on the recording, look at the chart.
It will help you hear when the tones of a melody move
mostly by step, mostly by leap, and mostly by repeated tones.

1. STEPS

2. REPEATS

3. LEAPS

4. STEPS

5. LEAPS

6. REPEATS

7. STEPS

Steps, Leaps, Repeats

Follow the notation as you listen to this song.
Can you find places where the tones repeat?
Move upward and downward by step?
Move by leap?

Winter Fun

Words and Music by Philip M. Slates

In the win - ter when the snow is ly - ing on the ground,

See the jol - ly sleigh, hear the sleigh bells' sound.

Out we go to run and play a - mong the drifts of snow;

Bring a - long your sled, to the hill we go.

Slid - ing, slid - ing down all in a world of white;

Slid - ing, slid - ing, hold _____ on tight.

Percussion Accompaniment

Add one of these parts to a performance of "Winter Fun."

Sleighbells

Tambourine

Woodblock

Listen for steps, leaps, and repeats in this dance from *Amahl and the Night Visitors.*

"Shepherds Dance" from

Amahl and the Night Visitors .... Menotti

Melodic Contour—
The Shape of a Melody

A melody can have tones that move upward or downward by step, tones that leap, and tones that repeat. The way tones move gives a melody its **contour,** or shape. How do the tones move in each phrase of this song?

Feasting by the Ocean

Song from Hawaii   Words by L. Golden

1. Sun is ris - ing o - ver the o - cean,

Breez - es set the palm ___ trees in mo - tion,

Time to rise and start the pre - par - a - tions,

For the day of feast - ing has be - gun.

2. Hurry now, the sun is rising higher,
   Dig the pit and start the fire.
   Fisher, bring your catch for cooking,
   Soon the time for feasting will be here.

3. Ready now, come gather round the table,
   Eat the *poi*, as much as you are able,
   Roasted pig is yours for the asking,
   Feasting by the ocean time is here.

Name-the-Tune Game

Here are the beginnings of some songs you may know. Can
you name each song by looking at the contour of the first phrase?

Same Contour–Different Levels

Follow the contour of the melody in each phrase as you listen to "I Love the Mountains."

I Love the Mountains

Traditional

Sequences–Same Pattern, Different Levels

Follow the contour of the melody as you listen to this song.
Notice especially the short melody patterns in the color boxes.
How are they alike? How are they different?

Music Alone Shall Live

Old German Round

I All things shall per - ish from un - der the sky;

II Mu - sic a - lone shall live, mu - sic a - lone shall live,

Mu - sic a - lone shall live, nev - er to die.

Pick a Part

You can add one of these parts to a performance of
"Music Alone Shall Live." Which part will you play?

Autoharp

Bell Part

A Pattern that Repeats

The nonsense syllables in this old American song imitate the sound of a spinning wheel.

Sarasponda

Early American Spinning Song

A C .... G₇ C

Sa - ra - spon - da, Sa - ra - spon - da, Sa - ra - spon - da, Ret - set - set!

B F .... C .... F .... C .... G₇

Ah - do - ray - oh! Ah - do-ray-boom-day-oh! Ah - do-ray-boom-day -

C .... G₇ C

ret - set - set! Aw - say - paw - say - oh!

Add a Harmony Part

One way to add harmony to a song is to sing an **ostinato**—a melody pattern that repeats.

Sing this ostinato throughout section A of "Sarasponda."

Ostinato for Section A

Boom - da, boom - da, boom - da, boom - da

Sing and Play an Ostinato

Play this pattern on a tambourine to accompany
the singing of this Hebrew folk song.

(shake)   :‖ Play throughout

Dundai

Hebrew Folk Song   English Words by Harold Aks

Land of Is - ra - el,   O   land   of   mine,

On   you   the   sun and moon and   stars   do   shine.

Dun - dai,   dun - dai,   dun - dai,   Dun - dai - dai,

Dun - dai,   dun - dai,   dun - dai,   Dun - dai - dai.

Sing this ostinato throughout section A.

Dun - dai, dun - dai, dun - dai, dun - dai

Play this ostinato during section B.

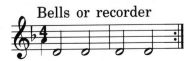
Bells or recorder

115

Partner Songs

Listen to the recording of two spirituals. One is printed
on this page, the other on the next page. Follow the music
of each song as you listen.

Now Let Me Fly

Black Spiritual

REFRAIN

Now let me fly, _____ Now let me fly, _____

Now let me fly _____ way up high, ___

Way in the mid-dle of the air.

VERSE

Way down yon-der in the mid-dle of the field,

See me work-ing at the char-iot wheel.

Not so par-tic-'lar 'bout work-ing at the wheel,

D.C. al Fine

But I just want to see how the char-iot feels.

Ezekiel Saw the Wheel

Black Spiritual

E - zek-iel saw the wheel,

'Way up in the mid-dle of the air.

E - zek-iel saw the wheel,

'Way in the mid-dle of the air.

Putting Two Songs Together

While some of your classmates sing "Ezekiel Saw the Wheel,"
others can sing the refrain of "Now Let Me Fly." Harmony
will be created when these **partner songs** are sung together.

Follow the Leader

Can you hear voices playing follow-the-leader in the recording of this song?

Follow Me ⑤

Traditional

Come a - long, Sing a song, Fol - low me; It is eas - y as you see. Ev - 'ry day, In this way, Just re - peat Till the tune's com - plete. _____

When your class can sing the melody of "Follow Me" without the recording, divide into two groups and try singing the song as a two-part round.

A Four-Part Round

In order to sing "Above the Plain" as a four-part round, you must be able to do two things well.

- Sing the melody without the recording.
- Keep the beat steady.

Above the Plain

Folk Song from Czechoslovakia

A - bove the plain of gold and green, A

young boy's head is plain - ly seen; A

hu - ya, hu - ya, hu - ya - ya, Swift - ly flow - ing riv - er; A

hu - ya, hu - ya, hu - ya - ya, Swift - ly flow - ing riv - er.

From SING ALONG THE WAY by permission of The Young Women's Christian Association of the USA.

Add this ostinato to the performance.

Bells

Eb   Bb   Eb

Countermelodies

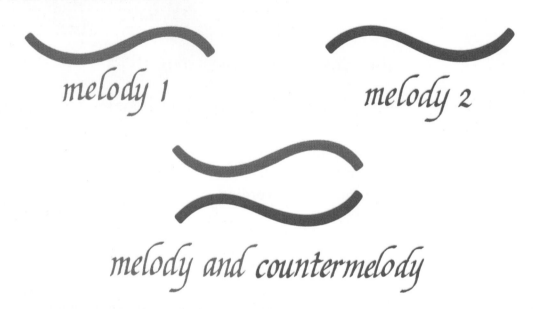

melody 1

melody 2

melody and countermelody

There are two different melodies in this song. Each one has a personality of its own. The two melodies can also be sung together to create harmony. When you listen to the recording for the first time, follow the part marked *melody* when you get to the refrain.

I Don't Mind 🔵

Words and Music by David Eddleman

Melody 1

I don't mind _ if you sing; _ I don't mind _

if you dance; _ I don't mind _ as long as

you don't mind _ if I should sing, _ too, just by chance. _

Melody 2

You'll nev-er go wrong keep-ing a song sing-ing a-long. You'll

see you've got to be hap-py and free sing-ing a mel-o-dy.

Melody

La la la — la la la, — La la la —

Countermelody

La la la la la la la la la la la la

la la la, — La la la — la la la la la la — la

la, La la la la la la la la la

La la la — la la la la, —

la la la. —

la la la la la la la, La la la la. —

Melody and Descant

You can create harmony by adding a **descant** to a melody.
A descant is a kind of countermelody that decorates the
main tune.

Listen for the descant when verse 2 is sung on the recording.
Notice how it weaves around the melody of the song—
sometimes sounding lower; more often sounding higher.

The Seasons

Words by Nancy Byrd Turner   Music by Jean Sibelius

1. The sea-sons come, the sea-sons go, And God has planned them all.

He makes the win-ter wind to blow, The au-tumn leaves to fall;

And when the balm-y spring-time De-scends on wood and hill,

His word goes forth, the leaves re-turn, And grass and bud and daf-fo-dil.

2. The weather is the plan of God;
   He sends the frost and snow,
   The pleasant rain upon the sod
   Where wheat and barley grow.
   And then the long year follows
   Like answer to His call,
   And ev'ry time is blessing time,
   For God has wisely planned them all!

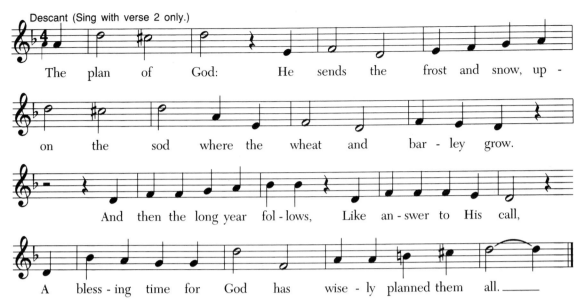

Descant (Sing with verse 2 only.)

The plan of God: He sends the frost and snow, up-

on the sod where the wheat and bar-ley grow.

And then the long year fol-lows, Like an-swer to His call,

A bless-ing time for God has wise-ly planned them all. ____

Harvest

I saw the farmer plough the field,
And row on row
The furrows grow.
I saw the farmer plough the field,
And hungry furrows grow.

I saw the farmer sow the wheat,
The golden grain,
In sun and rain.
I saw the farmer sow the wheat,
In shining sun and rain.

I saw at first a silvery sheen,
Then line on line
Of living green.
I saw at first a silvery sheen,
Then lines of living green.

The living green then turned to gold,
In thirty—fifty—
Hundred fold.
The living green then turned to gold
In mercies manifold.

M. M. Hutchinson

AB Form

Some songs have two
different sections. Can
you hear the two sections
in "Big Rock Candy Mountain"?

A

B

Big Rock Candy Mountain

American Folk Song

1. In the Big Rock Can - dy Moun - tain There's a land that's fair and
2. In the Big Rock Can - dy Moun - tain All the cows have wood - en

bright,   Where the hand - outs   grow   on   bush - es,   And you
legs,   And the bull - dogs   all   are   tooth - less,   And the

sleep   out   ev - 'ry   night;   Where the   box - cars   all   are
hens   lay   soft - boiled eggs,   All   the   trees   are   full   of

emp - ty,   And the sun shines ev - 'ry   day,   Oh, I'm
ap - ples, And the barns are   full   of   hay,   There's a

bound to go where there is - n't an - y snow, Where the rain does-n't fall and the
lake of stew and _ so - da pop, _ too, You can paddle all a-round in a

124

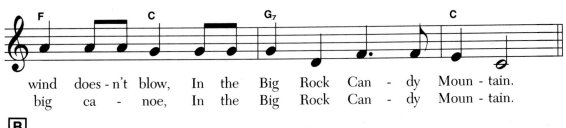

wind does-n't blow, In the Big Rock Can - dy Moun - tain.
big ca - noe, In the Big Rock Can - dy Moun - tain.

Oh, the buzz - in' of the bees in the syc - a - more trees Round the

so - da wa - ter foun - tain, Where the lem - on - ade springs and the

blue - bird sings In the Big Rock Can - dy Moun - tain.

Add a Part

Choose a percussion instrument and play this pattern throughout section A.

Play this pattern on a different percussion instrument throughout section B.

Listen for two different sections in this music by Bach. Name the form of the piece.

"Minuet" from
Notebook for Anna Magdalena Bach .... J.S. Bach

125

ABA Form

A   B   A

This song has two different sections—A and B. Listen to the music to find out what happens at the end of section B.

Open the Window, Noah 🅢

Three Different Sections

As you listen to the recording of "School Chant," follow the words of each section and tap the beat along with the snare drum.

(A) School was really great today;
I learned new things, had some time to play.

[B] Today we had rain, it looked dreary and grey;
But getting "A" on my test made it one bright day!

/C My friends and I played basketball;
I learned to multiply and felt ten feet tall!

You can use the A and B sections of "School Chant" to create a variety of forms; for example, ABA form.

(A) School was really great today;
I learned new things, had some time to play.

[B] Today we had rain, it looked dreary and grey;
But getting "A" on my test made it one bright day!

(A) School was really great today;
I learned new things, had some time to play.

Try saying the chant in these forms:

(A) [B] (A) [B]

(A) (A) [B] (A)

Now listen to the three sections of "School Chant" used in a longer form—a form called **rondo**.

 "School Chant" in Rondo Form

(A) [B] (A) /C\ (A)

Which section is repeated?

128

Rondo for Percussion

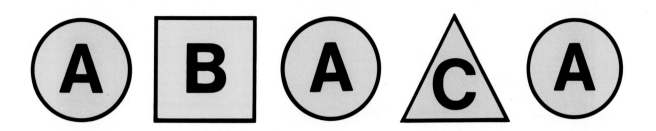

You can use the **rhythm** patterns below to create a rondo form. You will **need** to **choose three different patterns, one for** each section.

Listen for the rondo form in this piece. Do you know the name of the instrument that is playing?
Gigue en rondeau .... Rameau

Music for a Serenade

A CONCERT AT VAUXHALL (DETAIL)
DRAWN BY ROWLANDSON, AQUATINT

A serenade is music that is performed in the evening and usually out of doors. Serenades were popular in Mozart's time. Small groups of musicians sang or played at the palaces of rich noblemen to entertain the guests. There was also a custom of sending serenaders to a person's house on some special occasion. It was a nice way of greeting a returned traveler, or someone having a birthday. Composers were kept busy writing this "night music."

Mozart wrote a number of serenades. The most famous is the one he called *A Little Night Music.*

Imagine you are one of the palace guests as you listen to a piece from *A Little Night Music.*
"Romance" from *A Little Night Music* . . . . . **Mozart**

Three Themes from "Romance"

Theme A

Theme B

Theme C

Wolfgang Amadeus Mozart was born in the city of Salzburg, Austria, in 1756. He lived with his family in a comfortable old house that is now the famous Mozart Museum. When Mozart was only a little child of three, his father discovered that his son had unusual musical talent. And so he began to teach young Mozart how to play the clavier—an old keyboard instrument that looks like a tiny piano. The little boy was not satisfied with playing other people's music and began writing pieces of his own when he was four years old. Two years later Mozart played his music for kings and queens.

Although he lived only 35 years, Mozart composed a great deal of music in many different styles. His operas and symphonies are among the best-loved of all music.

Wolfgang Amadeus Mozart
(1756-1791)

Solo–One Voice

The broadway musical *The King and I* is about a lady named Anna who goes to teach the royal princes and princesses in the court of the king of Siam. Listen as Anna sings "I Whistle a Happy Tune."

I Whistle a Happy Tune 5
(from The King and I)

Words by Oscar Hammerstein II   Music by Richard Rodgers

When-ev-er I feel a - fraid   I hold my head e - rect   And
While shiv-er-ing in my shoes   I strike a care-less pose   And

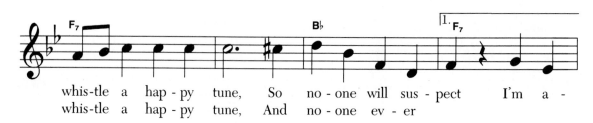

whis-tle a hap-py tune,   So no-one will sus-pect   I'm a-
whis-tle a hap-py tune,   And no-one ev-er

fraid. _____   knows   I'm a - fraid. _____   The re-

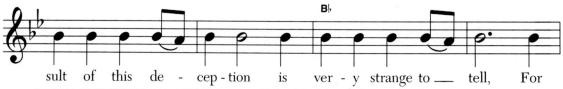

sult of this de - cep-tion is ver-y strange to __ tell,   For

when I fool the peo-ple I fear, I fool my-self as well! I

whis-tle a hap-py tune And ev-'ry sin-gle time The

hap-pi-ness in the tune con-vin-ces me that I'm not a-fraid.

Coda

Make be-lieve you're brave And the trick will take you far.

You may be as brave as you make be-lieve you are.

Whistle _____

You may be as brave as you make be-lieve you

are. _____

Solo and Chorus

In this song, Sir Joseph explains how he got his job as admiral of the British navy. Join in on the chorus parts when you can.

When I Was a Lad

From "Pinafore"   Words by W. S. Gilbert   Music by Arthur Sullivan

1. When I was a lad I served a term As of-fice
2. As of-fice boy I made such a mark That they gave me the

boy to an at-tor-ney's firm, I cleaned the win-dows and I swept the
post of a jun-ior clerk, I served the writs with a smile so

floor, And I pol-ished up the han-dle on the big front door.
bland, And I cop-ied all the let-ters in a big round hand.

Chorus

And he pol-ished up the han-dle on the big front door.
And he cop-ied all the let-ters in a big round hand.

Solo

I pol-ished up that han-dle so care-ful-lee } That now I am the
I cop-ied all the let-ters in a hand so free }

134

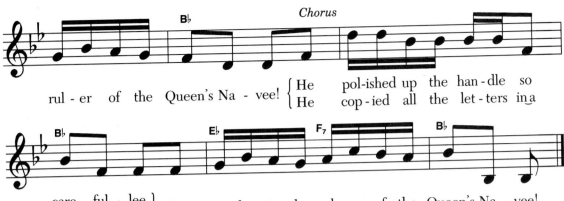

rul - er of the Queen's Na - vee!
{ He pol-ished up the han-dle so
He cop-ied all the let-ters in a }

care - ful - lee
hand so free
} That now he is the rul - er of the Queen's Na - vee!

3. In serving writs I made such a name,
   That an articled clerk I soon became;
   I wore clean collars and a bran' new suit
   For the pass examination at the Institute.
   For the pass examination at the Institute.
   And that pass examination did so well for me,
   That now I am the ruler of the Queen's Navee!
   And that pass examination did so well for he,
   That now he is the ruler of the Queen's Navee!

4. Of legal knowledge I acquired such a grip,
   That they took me into the partnership,
   And that junior partnership I ween
   Was the only ship that I ever had seen,
   Was the only ship that he ever had seen.
   But that kind of ship so suited me,
   That now I am the ruler of the Queen's Navee!
   But that kind of ship so suited he,
   That now he is the ruler of the Queen's Navee!

5. I grew so rich that I was sent
   By a pocket borough into Parliament;
   I always voted at my party's call,
   And I never thought of thinking for myself at all.
   And he never thought of thinking for himself at all.
   I thought so little they rewarded me,
   By making me the ruler of the Queen's Navee!
   He thought so little they rewarded he,
   By making him the ruler of the Queen's Navee!

6. Now landsmen all, whoever you may be,
   If you want to rise to the top of the tree,
   If your soul isn't fettered to an office stool,
   Be careful to be guided by this golden rule,
   Be careful to be guided by this golden rule:
   Stick close to your desks and never go to sea,
   And you all may be rulers of the Queen's Navee!
   Stick close to your desks and never go to sea,
   And you all may be rulers of the Queen's Navee!

A Combination of Voices

You can hear examples of solo voices on the recordings of the songs on pages 132 and 134.

• "I Whistle a Happy Tune" is sung by a woman.
• "When I Was a Lad" is sung by a man.

Voices can also sing together in many different combinations.

 Listen for the voices in this recording of "America, the Beautiful." How many voices do you hear?
America, the Beautiful, Version 1

 Here is another version of "America, the Beautiful." Who is singing in this version? How many voices do you hear?
America, the Beautiful, Version 2

 On this recording you will hear another combination of voices. Do you hear many voices or few voices in this version of the song?
America, the Beautiful, Version 3

Can you finish these sentences?

• A combination of two voices singing in parts is called a

_____.

• A combination of three voices singing in parts is called a

_____.

• A combination of many voices singing in parts is called a

_____.

Duet

Trio

Chorus

The Sound of an Orchestra

An orchestra is made up of four families of instruments. Can you name an instrument from each of these families?

- Woodwinds

- Brass

- Strings

- Percussion

In the photograph below, find instruments that belong to each of the four families.

One of the pieces you might hear at an orchestra concert is
"Russian Sailor's Dance" by the composer Glière. He based the
composition on this old Russian folk song.

Theme

 Listen for all the families of instruments as they play
together in this composition.
"Russian Sailor's Dance" from
The Red Poppy . . . . Glière

The Sound of String Instruments

The violin, viola, cello, and string bass are members of the string family. Although their shapes are similar, their sizes vary from small to very large.

The string instruments are usually bowed. The sound is produced by drawing a bow across the strings. The pitch is low if the string is long and heavy, higher if the string is shorter and lighter.

Look at the pictures of the four instruments.
• Which instrument plays the lowest tones?
• Which instrument plays the highest tones?
• How do you know?

Listen for the instruments of the string family in an arrangement of a song from your book.
"We Gather Together" for Strings

string bass

cello

viola

violin

The Sound of Woodwind Instruments

The flute, oboe, clarinet, and bassoon are members of the woodwind family. All the instruments of this family were originally made of wood. Today the flute and sometimes the clarinet are made of metal or other material.

The woodwind instruments are played by blowing across or into the tube of the instrument. The air column inside the tube is set in vibration and tones are produced. Different pitches are created by changing the length of the column of air. The pitch is low if the column of air is long, higher if the column of air is shorter.

Look at the pictures of the instruments.
• Which instrument produces the lowest tones?
• Which instrument produces the highest tones?
• How do you know?

Listen for the instruments of the woodwind family in this arrangement of "We Gather Together."
"We Gather Together" for Woodwinds

bassoon

clarinet

oboe

flute

The Sound of Brass Instruments

The trumpet, trombone, French horn, and tuba are members of the brass family. They are sometimes called brass wind instruments because the player blows into a mouthpiece to create the tone.

Each instrument consists of a long metal tube with a mouthpiece at one end and a bell-shaped opening at the other. The pitch is low if the tube is long. The pitch is high if the tube is short.

Look at the pictures of the instruments.
• Which instrument plays the lowest tones?
• Which instrument plays the highest tones?
• How do you know?

 Listen for the instruments of the brass family in this arrangement of "We Gather Together."
"We Gather Together" for Brass

144

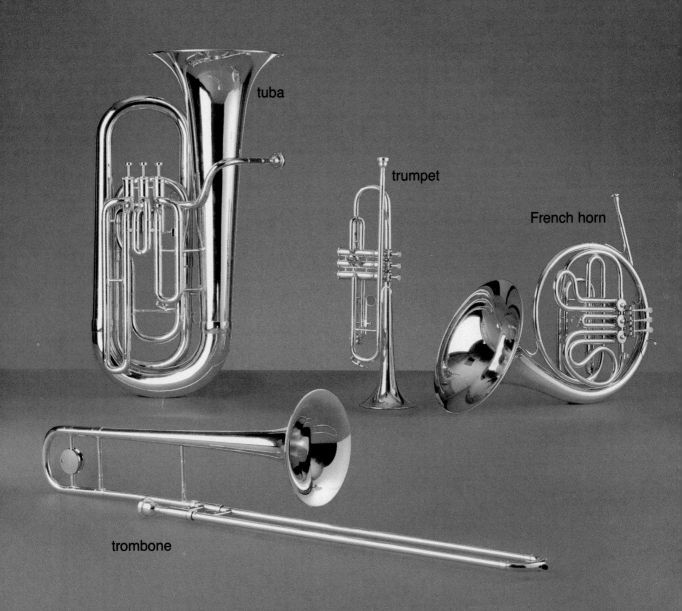

tuba

trumpet

French horn

trombone

The Sound of Percussion

The members of the percussion family come in many different shapes and sizes. They are all played by being struck with sticks, hammers, or hands, or by being shaken.

What classroom percussion are played by striking? By shaking? Experiment.

Listen for the instruments of the percussion family in this piece by a famous Mexican composer. The instruments he used are pictured in your book.

Toccata for Percussion .... Chávez

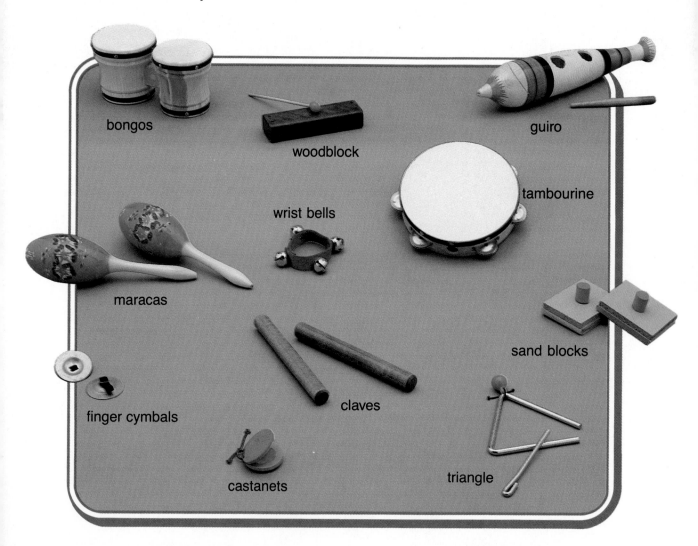

bongos

woodblock

guiro

wrist bells

tambourine

maracas

sand blocks

finger cymbals

claves

castanets

triangle

chimes

gong

cymbal

bass drum

xylophone

snare drum

timpani

orchestra bells

hand cymbals

The Sound of a Concert Band

Band music has always been popular in our country. In the early 1900s, going to the Sunday band concert in the park was a favorite pastime.

Today, in the fall, high school and college marching bands all over America perform during halftime at football games. Band music may also be heard in concert halls.

A concert band is made up of wind instruments and percussion. Can you identify any of the instruments in the concert band shown in the photograph below?

One of the pieces you might hear at a band concert is *Folk Song Suite*.

The composer, Ralph Vaughan Williams, used this English folk song in one part of the piece.

 "March" from *Folk Song Suite* . . . . Vaughan Williams

Can you hear meter in music? You will hear seven songs
from your book. As you listen to each song, decide whether
the beats are moving in sets of two or in sets of three. If
the beats move in twos, circle METER IN 2 on your
worksheet. If the beats move in threes, circle METER IN 3.

1.   METER IN 2   METER IN 3

2.   METER IN 2   METER IN 3

3.   METER IN 2   METER IN 3

4.   METER IN 2   METER IN 3

5.   METER IN 2   METER IN 3

6.   METER IN 2   METER IN 3

7.   METER IN 2   METER IN 3

What Do You Hear  4   Meter

You will hear parts of seven instrumental pieces. Each
time a number is called, decide whether the music moves
in a meter of 2 or a meter of 3. Listen, then circle your
answer on your worksheet.

1.   METER IN 2   METER IN 3

2.   METER IN 2   METER IN 3

3.   METER IN 2   METER IN 3

4.   METER IN 2   METER IN 3

5.   METER IN 2   METER IN 3

6.   METER IN 2   METER IN 3

7.   METER IN 2   METER IN 3

You will hear seven melodies. Listen particularly for the ending of each melody. If the tones move upward at the end of the melody, circle the word UPWARD on your worksheet. If the tones move downward, circle the word DOWNWARD.

1.   UPWARD   DOWNWARD

2.   UPWARD   DOWNWARD

3.   UPWARD   DOWNWARD

4.   UPWARD   DOWNWARD

5.   UPWARD   DOWNWARD

6.   UPWARD   DOWNWARD

7.   UPWARD   DOWNWARD

You will hear seven melodies played on a synthesizer. Each time a number is called, decide whether the tones in the melody move mostly by step, mostly by leap, or mostly by repeated tones. Listen, then circle your answer on your worksheet.

1.   STEP   LEAP   REPEAT

2.   STEP   LEAP   REPEAT

3.   STEP   LEAP   REPEAT

4.   STEP   LEAP   REPEAT

5.   STEP   LEAP   REPEAT

6.   STEP   LEAP   REPEAT

7.   STEP   LEAP   REPEAT

Test 3 ✓

Find the line at the right that matches the shape, or
contour, of the melody at the left. On your worksheet,
write the letter of the line in the blank.

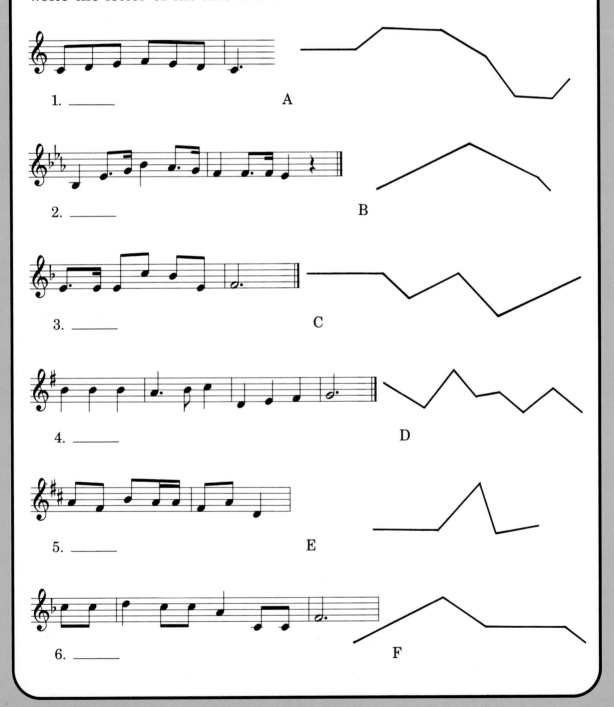

1. _____

A

2. _____

B

3. _____

C

4. _____

D

5. _____

E

6. _____

F

Test 4 ✓

Read the sentences, and on your worksheet, fill in the blanks with the correct word or words from the list below.

round   countermelodies

unison   ostinato

partner songs   descant

1. When everyone in the group sings the same melody at the same time, we say the group is singing in _____.

2. When half the group sings one song, and at the same time, the other half sings a different song, we call these two independent songs _____ _____.

3. When two or more groups sing the same song, each group starting at a different time, we call this follow-the-leader song a _____.

4. When a small group sings a harmony part that decorates the melody (often sounding above the melody), we call this harmony part a _____.

5. When a short melody pattern is repeated over and over to accompany a song, we call this harmony part an ____.

6. When two melodies from the same song are sung together, they are called _____.

A. What is the form shown in each example below?

1. ___A___   _____   _____

2. ___A___   _____   _____   _____

3. ___A___   _____   _____   _____

4. ___A___   _____   _____   _____   _____

B. The form of each song listed below is either AB or ABA. Look through the music, and on your worksheet, write the name of the form in the blank. Use the song index in your book to find the page number of each song.

    1. "As the Sun Goes Down" _____

    2. "Open the Window, Noah" _____

    3. "Skye Boat Song" _____

    4. "Columbia, the Gem of the Ocean" _____

    5. "Now Let Me Fly" _____

    6. "Cindy" _____

What Do You Hear ? 7   Voices

You will hear six selections. When a number is called, decide who is singing. Listen, then circle your answer on your worksheet.

1. child

children

woman

man

men and women

2. child

children

woman

man

men and women

3. child

children

woman

man

men and women

4. child

children

woman

man

men and women

5. child

children

woman

man

men and women

6. child

children

woman

man

men and women

Test 6 ✓

A. Write the name of each instrument in the correct family.

violin	flute	trombone	bassoon
claves	viola	cymbals	maracas
trumpet	clarinet	oboe	tuba
string bass	cello	French horn	drum

STRING

1. _____
2. _____
3. _____
4. _____

WOODWINDS

1. _____
2. _____
3. _____
4. _____

BRASS

1. _____
2. _____
3. _____
4. _____

PERCUSSION

1. _____
2. _____
3. _____
4. _____

B. Read The sentences below. Write *T* if the sentence is true. Write *F* if the sentence is false.

1. String instruments are usually played with a bow. _____

2. Woodwind and brass instruments are played by blowing. _____

3. The instrument of the brass family that plays the lowest tones is the trumpet. _____

4. A tambourine can be played by striking and shaking. _____

You will hear six examples of instrumental music. When a number is called, decide which group of instruments is playing. Listen, then circle your answer on your worksheet.

1. orchestra

strings

woodwinds

brass

percussion

band

2. orchestra

strings

woodwinds

brass

percussion

band

3. orchestra

strings

woodwinds

brass

percussion

band

4. orchestra

strings

woodwinds

brass

percussion

band

5. orchestra

strings

woodwinds

brass

percussion

band

6. orchestra

strings

woodwinds

brass

percussion

band

SHARING MUSIC

Music Creates a Mood

Felix Mendelssohn composed a group of pieces to accompany William Shakespeare's play *A Midsummer Night's Dream*. The piece Mendelssohn wrote to be performed between the first and second acts of the play is called "Scherzo."

As you listen to the piece, look at the words in the two lists below. Which list of words suggests the mood, or feeling of the music—the first list or the second list?

light	heavy
excited	calm
bright	dark
merry	melancholy
lively	dull

"Scherzo" from *A Midsummer Night's Dream* .... *Mendelssohn*

164

When Mendelssohn's "Scherzo" is played again, listen for the
two main themes. Can you hear which theme is introduced by
woodwind instruments and which is played by string
instruments?

Theme 1

Theme 2

Felix Mendelssohn
(1809-1847)

Felix Mendelssohn was born into a
happy, music-loving family in Germany
in 1809. Both he and his sister showed
early signs of great musical talent. Their
mother gave them their first music les-
sons; soon they were ready for further
study with the best teachers that could
be found. Felix made wonderful progress
and began to write music when he was
ten years old.

As Felix was growing up there were
many musical parties in the Mendelssohn home where famous musicians and
artists of the day gathered for Sunday
evening concerts. The program always
contained one or more compositions by
the young Mendelssohn, including one of
the pieces from *A Midsummer Night's
Dream.*

Round and Round

Girls and boys all over the world enjoy singing rounds. Each round on this page comes from a different country. One comes from Germany, the other tune comes from Hungary.

Love Is Like a Ring
(Liebe ist ein Ring)

Traditional Round from Germany

Love is like a ring. ____ A ring has ___ no end - ing.
Lie - be ist ein Ring. ____ Ein Ring hat ___ kein En - de.

Bells or soprano xylophone

I'll Begin Ahead of You

Folk Tune from Hungary

I'll be - gin a - head of you, You'll be - gin be - hind me;
I will stay a - head of you, And you will not find me.

Bells or soprano xylophone

Tempo and Performance

Look at the word in the color box. Do you know what it means? It tells you how this song should be sung.

Stars of the Heavens
(Las estrellitas del cielo)

Folk Song from Mexico   English Version by Aura Kontra

Stars of the heav-ens are wink - ing, With sil - v'ry light they are
Las es - tre - lli - tas del cie - lo Bri - llan con su luz de

twin - kling. A heav-en - ly rid - er came jing - ling
pla - ta. _____ San - tia - go las fué sem - bran - do

With sil - v'ry spurs, star - light sprin - kling.
Con sus es - pue - las de pla - ta.

Classroom Orchestra

Which of these parts will you choose to play in a performance of "Stars of the Heavens"?

Autoharp   Play throughout.

Maracas   Play throughout.

Bells

Ostinatos to Sing and Play

Think of all the bell sounds you have ever heard.
What did the bells tell you?

The Carillon
(Le Carillon)

Traditional Round

Oh, hear the ring - ing car - il - lon,
En - ten - dez vous le car - il - lon,

Di - ri don, don, don, don, don, don, don, don, don, don.
Di - ri don, don, don, don, don, don, don, don, don, don.

Ostinatos

Which of these ostinatos will you choose to accompany the song?
Will you sing it? Play it on bells?

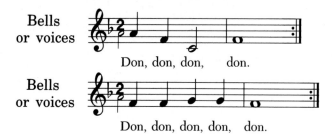

Bells
or voices

Don, don, don, don.

Bells
or voices

Don, don, don, don, don.

Listen for this ostinato pattern in a piece by the French
composer Georges Bizet.

LISTENING SKILLS 7

"Carillon" from *L'Arlésienne Suite No. 1* ..... Bizet

168

A Bell Song from China

Some Chinese music is over 4000 years old. It can be traced back centuries before the Great Wall of China was built.

Which instrument will you choose to accompany this Chinese folk song?

Golden Bells

Folk Song from China

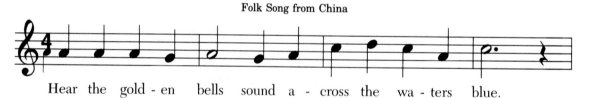

Hear the gold-en bells sound a-cross the wa-ters blue.

Gen-tle winds that blow sing their sweet __ song for you;

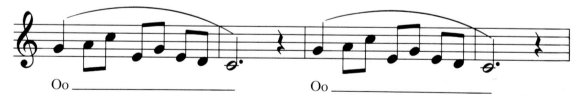

Oo _____ Oo _____

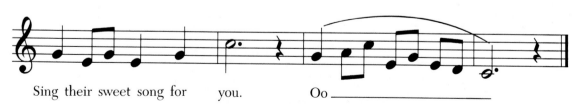

Sing their sweet song for you. Oo _____

From *New Dimensions in Music*, Book 4 © 1970 American Book Company. Reprinted by permission of D.C. Heath and Company.

Add an Accompaniment

Mallet Instruments

Bell Part 1

Bell Part 2

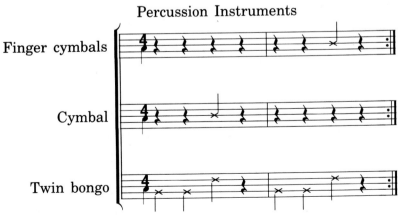

Percussion Instruments

Finger cymbals

Cymbal

Twin bongo

A Special Sound from Japan

The instrument shown in the picture is called a *koto*. It is one of the most popular instruments in Japan. Listen for the special sound of the koto on the recording of "Sakura."

Sakura 7

Folk Song from Japan   Modern Arrangement by Henry Burnett
English Version by Lorene Hoyt

1. Sa - ku - ra,   Sa - ku - ra,   Cher - ry   blos - soms
2. Sa - ku - ra,   Sa - ku - ra,   Blos - soms   wav - ing
   Sa - ku - ra,   Sa - ku - ra,   Ya - yo - i   no

ev - 'ry - where.   Clouds   of   glo - ry   fill   the __ sky,
in   the __ breeze.   Yo - shi - no,   the   cher - ry __ land,
so - ra __ wa,   Mi - wa - ta - su   ka - gi - ri,

Mist   of   beau - ty   in   the __ air,   Love - ly   col - ors   float - ing __ by,
Tat - su - ta,   the   ma - ple __ trees,   Ka - ra - sa - ki,   pine   tree __ grand,
Ka - su - mi   ka   ku - mo - ka,   Ni - o - i   zo   i - zu - ru;

Sa - ku - ra,   Sa - ku - ra,   Let __ all   come _ sing - ing.
Sa - ku - ra,   Sa - ku - ra,   Let __ all   come _ sing - ing.
I - za - ya,   i - za - ya   Mi __ ni   yu - kan. ____

Here is a percussion part to play as an accompaniment for "Sakura." Play it over and over all through the song.

Drum ostinato

You might want to try playing this bell part when the class
sings the song.

Countermelody for bells or recorder

One Voice– Many Voices

How will you use your voice when you sing this "dum dum diddeley" song?

Hey, Dum Diddeley Dum 🎵7

Words and Music by Marc Stone

Refrain Hey, dum did - dle - ley dum, _____
1. Ev - 'ry - one gath - er round, _____

Hey, dum did - dle - ley dum, _____
Hey, dum did - dle - ley dum, _____

Hey, dum did - dle - ley, Hey dum did - dle - ley,
'Cause we just found this brand new sound, It's a

Hey, dum did - dle - ley dum. _____
Hey, dum did - dle - ley dum. _____ *Refrain*

2. Come and join in the fun,
   Hey, dum diddleley dum,
   We're gonna sing till the day is done,
   Hey, dum diddleley dum. *Refrain*

3. Ev'ryone come and sing,
   Hey, dum diddleley dum,
   We're gonna make these old rafters ring,
   Hey, dum diddleley dum. *Refrain*

Add a Harmony Part

In which direction do the tones move in this bell part?

Line up the bells from low C to high C. Play the bell part to accompany the song.

Add Another Harmony Part

Here is another part to sing with "Hey Dum Diddeley Dum."

Hey, dum did-de-ley dum, —

Hey, dum did-de-ley dum, —

Hey, dum did-de-ley, Hey, dum did-de-ley,

Hey, dum did-de-ley dum. —

Be a Story Teller

Pretend you are reading the story of Señor Don Gato to a kindergarten class. Think of interesting ways to use your *speaking* voice to make the story exciting.

Now use your *singing* voice to tell the story.

Don Gato 7

Folk Song from Mexico English Words by Margaret Marks

1. Oh, Se - ñor Don Ga - to was a cat, _____
2. "I a - dore you!" wrote the la - dy cat, _____

On a high, red roof Don Ga - to sat. _____
Who was fluff - y, white, and nice and fat. _____

He went there to read a let - ter,
There was not a sweet - er kit - ty, meow, meow, meow,

Where the read - ing light was bet - ter,
In the coun - try or the cit - y, meow, meow, meow,

'Twas a love note for Don Ga - to! _____
And she said she'd wed Don Ga - to! _____

176

3. Oh, Don Gato jumped so happily
   He fell off the roof and broke his knee,
   Broke his ribs and all his whiskers, . . .
   And his little solar plexus, . . .
   "¡Ay carramba!" cried Don Gato!

4. Then the doctors all came on the run
   Just to see if something could be done,
   And they held a consultation, . . .
   About how to save their patient, . . .
   How to save Señor Don Gato!

5. But in spite of everything they tried
   Poor Señor Don Gato up and died,
   Oh, it wasn't very merry, . . .
   Going to the cemetery, . . .
   For the ending of Don Gato!

6. When the funeral passed the market
      square
   Such a smell of fish was in the air,
   Though his burial was slated, . . .
   He became re-animated! . . .
   He came back to life, Don Gato!

Here is a poem about another cat—a proud and
mysterious cat.

The Mysterious Cat

I saw a proud mysterious cat,
I saw a proud mysterious cat,
Too proud to catch a mouse or rat—
   Mew, mew, mew.

But catnip she would eat and purr,
But catnip she would eat and purr,
And goldfish she did much prefer—
   Mew, mew, mew.

I saw a cat—'twas but a dream,
I saw a cat—'twas but a dream,
Who scorned the slave that brought her cream—
   Mew, mew, mew.

Unless the slave were dressed in style,
Unless the slave were dressed in style,
And knelt before her all the while—
   Mew, mew, mew.

Did you ever hear of a thing like that?
Did you ever hear of a thing like that?
Did you ever hear of a thing like that?
Oh, what a proud mysterious cat.
Oh, what a proud mysterious cat.
Oh, what a proud mysterious cat.
   Mew . . . . Mew . . . . Mew.

Vachel Lindsay

177

A Highland Rowing Song

Skye is one of the Hebrides Islands, located west of Scotland. This old highland rowing song tells about Bonnie Prince Charlie (Charles Edward Stuart). He was "born to be king," but was defeated in the Battle of Culloden Moor and escaped by boat to the island of Skye.

As you listen to the music, feel the strong pull on the oars as the boat is pushed through the water.

(A) REFRAIN

Skye Boat Song

Words by Sir Harold Boulton   Music by Annie MacLeod

Speed, bon - nie boat, like a bird on the wing;

"On - ward," the sail - ors cry.

Car - ry the lad that's born to be king,

O - ver the sea to Skye.

B VERSE

1. Loud the winds howl, loud the waves roar,
2. Tho' the waves leap, soft shall ye sleep,

Thun - der - clouds rend the air; _____
O - cean's a roy - al bed. _____

Baf - fled, our foes stand by the shore;
Rock'd in the deep, Flo - ra will keep

D.C. al Fine

Fol - low they will not dare. _____
Watch by your wea - ry head. _____

Bell Accompaniments

Which bell part will you play to accompany "Skye Boat Song"?

Words and Music

There are all kinds of songs in your book—ballads, nonsense songs, shanties. What kind of song do you think "Raisins and Almonds" is? The words may give you a hint.

Raisins and Almonds

Jewish Folk Song   English Words by Sylvia and John Kolb

To my lit - tle one's cra - dle in the night, _____

Comes a new lit - tle goat _____ snow - y white. _____

The goat will trot to the mar - ket, _____

While moth - er her watch _____ will keep, _____

To bring you back rai - sins and al - monds. ___

Sleep, my lit - tle one, sleep. _____

Play one of these parts as an introduction to "Raisins and Almonds."

Lullaby Tunes

Lullabies are sung all over the world. "Raisins and Almonds," for example, comes from the Middle East. Here are a few lullaby tunes from other parts of the world. Try playing one of them on the bells.

Berceuse (bear-SOOS) is a French word meaning "lullaby." Listen for the gentle rocking movement in this piece called "Berceuse."

"Berceuse" from *Dolly* .... Fauré

Friendly Faces

Think of all the friendly faces you have seen as you listen to "No One Like You." The song tells you about some of the things that make each one of us special.

No One Like You

Words and Music by Andra Willis Muhoberac

I think you're great,   I real - ly do;   I'm glad to
know some-one as nice as you.   I like your smile,   it's real - ly
you,   I like the things — you say and do.   There's not a
sin - gle soul who sees the skies the way you see them through your
eyes,   And aren't you glad?   You should be glad there's
no one,   no one _____ ex - act - ly like you. _____

Ring Around the World

Ring around the world
Taking hands together
All across the temperate
And the torrid weather.
Past the royal palm-trees
By the ocean sand
Making a ring around the world
Taking each other's hand;
In the valleys, on the hill,
Over the prairie spaces,
There's a ring around the world
Made of children's friendly faces.

Annette Wynne

A Song in Folk-Rock Style

As you listen to this song, keep time
to the soft-rock movement of the music
with his pattern.

Pat clap clap clap, Pat clap clap clap

Sun Magic

Words and Music by Donovan Leitch

1. The   sun   is   a ver - y mag - ic   fel - low,
2. The   wind   is   a ver - y fick - le   fel - low,
3. The   rain   is   a ver - y sad____   la - dy,

He   shines   down   on me each   day - ay - ay - ay.____
He   blows   all   my dreams a -   way - ay - ay - ay.____
She   falls   down   on me some - times,_____

The   sun   is   a ver - y mag - ic   fel - low,
The   wind   is   a ver - y fick - le   fel - low,
The   rain   is   a ver - y sad____   la - dy,

He   shines   down   on me   all day   -   ay - ay - ay, ____
𝄆 Blow - in' all my dreams a - way   -   ay - ay - ay, ____
She   falls   down   on me   some - times, _____

He shines down on me each day. _____
7 Blow - in' all my dreams a - way. _____
She falls down on me some - times. _____

4. The sea is a very, very old man,
   Deeper than the deepest blue,
   The sea is a very, very old man,
   Deeper than the deepest blue,
   Deeper than the deepest blue.

5. The moon is a typical lady,
   I watch her wax and wane,
   The moon is a typical lady,
   I watch her wax and wane,
   I watch her wax and wane.

6. A star is so very far away, love,
   Just between you and me,
   A star is so very far away, love,
   Just between you and me,
   Just between you and me.

Add a Part

Autoharp and bells

You will hear four sets of pieces. In each set, one piece is in a slow tempo, the other, in a fast tempo. Listen to both pieces, decide which is slow and which is fast, then circle your answers on your worksheet.

1. First piece   SLOW   FAST

    Second piece   SLOW   FAST

2. First piece   SLOW   FAST

    Second piece   SLOW   FAST

3. First piece   SLOW   FAST

    Second piece   SLOW   FAST

4. First piece   SLOW   FAST

    Second piece   SLOW   FAST

What Do You Hear 10   Style

A good accompaniment fits the style and mood of a song.
Listen to five songs. You will hear two accompaniments for
each song. Which accompaniment do you think suits the
song best? Listen to both accompaniments, then circle your
answer on your worksheet.

1. Song: "You're a Grand Old Flag"

    Accompaniment 1   Accompaniment 2

2. Song: "Goodnight"

    Accompaniment 1   Accompaniment 2

3. Song: "The Dreamer"

    Accompaniment 1   Accompaniment 2

4. Song: "Oh, Susanna"

    Accompaniment 1   Accompaniment 2

5. Song: "Yankee Doodle Boy"

    Accompaniment 1   Accompaniment 2

A. In music, certain symbols are used to tell a performer how loud or how soft to sing and play. Draw a line between each symbol in the left column and its definition in the right column.

1.	*p*	getting louder
2.	*mf*	loud
3.	*mp*	getting softer
4.	*f*	moderately soft
5.	<	soft
6.	>	moderately loud

B. The words in each of the following lists suggests an appropriate style of performance for some songs in your book. Look through the songs listed below and decide which list suits the style of each song. Write the letter *A* or *B* in the blank. Use the song index in your book to find the page number of each song.

A	B
lively	calmly
vigorously	smoothly
briskly	leisurely

1. "You're a Grand Old Flag" _____

2. "Stars of the Heavens" _____

3. "Donkey Riding" _____

4. "Barges" _____

5. "Raisins and Almonds" _____

6. "Some Folks" _____

Test 8 ✓

Read the sentences below. On your worksheet, write *T* in the blank if the sentence is true. Write *F* in the blank if the sentence is false.

1. To sing a song expressively, you must consider the meaning of the words. _____

2. As each part of a round is added, the texture gets thinner. _____

3. Rounds are only sung in America. _____

4. An ostinato is a pattern that is repeated over and over again. _____

5. A koto is an instrument that is popular in Japan. _____

6. A lullaby should be sung loud and fast. _____

7. A song that tells a story is called a *ballad.* _____

8. An instrument part that starts before a song is sung is called an *introduction.* _____

9. A coda comes at the end of a piece. _____

10. The songs "Goodnight" and "Yankee Doodle Boy" should be sung in exactly the same way. _____

Greeter: Hi! My name is (   ). Welcome to *Only Love Is Spoken Here*—a musical program presented by (Mrs. Jones's fourth grade class). You won't see any scenery—only love; no costumes—only love. There isn't any story line—only love. So if you're bitter, pessimistic, angry, selfish—OUTSIDE! Only love is spoken here!

Only Love Is Spoken Here

Words and Music by Carmino Ravosa

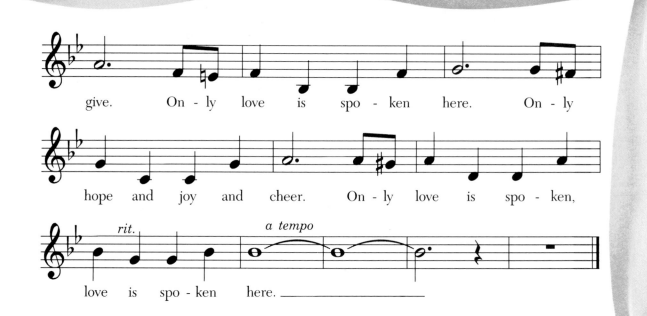

give. On - ly love is spo - ken here. On - ly

hope and joy and cheer. On - ly love is spo - ken,

rit. *a tempo*

love is spo - ken here. _____

Student 1: Love—L-O-V-E—only four letters, but it's a *big* word. A lot of people have their own idea about what it means.

Student 2: Albert Schweitzer said that as long as there are people in the world who are hungry, sick, lonely, or living in fear, they are my responsibility. That is love.

Student 3: Robert Frost said, "We love the things we love for what they are."

Student 4: Someone once said, "Love is not getting, but giving— it is goodness, honor, and peace."

Student 5: And speaking of peace and goodness, have you looked at the newspaper lately? There's a lot of poverty, hunger, and crime out there. I wish more people would care about one another—be givers, not takers. Let's sing about how it *should* be— that's what our play is all about.

Let's Sing About You

Words and Music by Carmino Ravosa

Let's sing a-bout you, Let's sing a-bout me, Let's

sing a-bout things we feel and we see. Let's sing a-bout you, Let's

sing a-bout me, Let's sing a-bout things the way they should be. Let's

sing a-bout a world that's al-ways hap-py, Sing a-bout a world that's al-ways fair,

Sing a-bout a world that's al-ways giv-ing, Sing a-bout a world where peo-ple care. —

Chorus / *Solo*

— So let's — So let's sing a-bout you, Let's

sing a-bout me, Let's sing a-bout things the way they should be.

Student 6: I guess before we try to change the whole world we've got to like ourselves first—starting with the way that we look.

Student 7: It's amazing how many kids don't like the way they look.

Student 8: But not us! Right?

Students 6 and 7: Right!

I Like the Way That I Look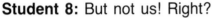

Words and Music by Carmino Ravosa

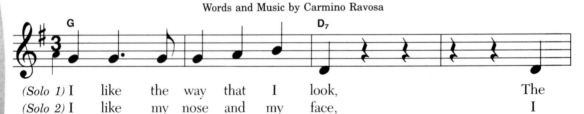

(Solo 1) I like the way that I look, The
(Solo 2) I like my nose and my face, I

things from my par-ents I took.
take them with me ev-'ry place.
I like the way that I,

I like the way that I, I like the way that I look.

(Solos 1,2)
Don't get me wrong, I'm not per-fect.   Faults, I've got me a
can't judge a book by its cov-er,   We're all a one of a

few.   But I'll nev-er let them stop me   from
kind.   There's beau-ty in all of us,   You

do-ing what I want to do. _____ (Solo 3)   I like the way that I
just got to look and you'll find. _____ (Solos 1,2,3)   I like my-self, I like

am.   And all oth-er feel-ings can scram.
me.   There's no one that I'd rath-er be.

I like the way that I,   I like the way that I,   I like the

way that I look.   (Chorus) You   (Chorus) I like the way that I,

I like the way that I,   I like the way that I look.   I look!

(Shout)
(3 Solos)

Student 9: How you look on the outside isn't all that important—it's what's on the inside that counts. So stop knocking yourself—in fact, do the opposite—be good to yourself!

Be Good to Yourself 🎵

Words and Music by Carmino Ravosa

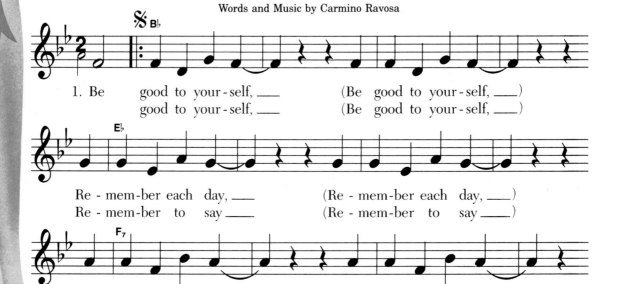

1. Be   good to your-self, ___   (Be   good to your-self, ___)
    good to your-self, ___   (Be   good to your-self, ___)

Re - mem-ber each   day, ___   (Re - mem-ber each   day, ___)
Re - mem-ber   to   say ___   (Re - mem-ber   to   say ___)

That work-ing   is   fine, ___   (That work-ing   is   fine, ___)
A   few words of   praise ___   (A   few words of   praise ___)

But don't for-get play. ___ (But don't for-get play. ___) 2. Be

To your-self ev-'ry day. ___ (To your-self ev-'ry day. __

__) Re - mem-ber to laugh, ___ To sing and have fun. ___

Do a lit-tle of each ___ be-fore each day is done. ___

Slower, 2nd time

Be good to your-self, ___ (Be good to your-self, ___)

What ev - er you do, ___ (What ev - er you do, ___)

You don't want to hurt ___ (You don't want to hurt ___)

The per-son called you. (The per-son called you.) "Now everybody echo!"

D.S. (with repeat) al *rit.*

1. Be per - son called you.)

199

Student 10: Hey, that sure was good singing.

Student 9: Thank you.

Student 10: What did you say?

Student 9: I said, "Thank you."

Student 11: That's very nice! Sometimes we show our love in very simple ways—like saying "Thank you." "Thank you for helping me carry my packages." "Thank you for holding the door." "Thank you for being my friend." And do you know what my answer to any "Thank you" is? It's saying "Thank you for saying 'Thank you.'"

Thank You for Saying "Thank You"

Words and Music by Carmino Ravosa

Thank you ____ for say - ing "thank you," That's a
thank you ____ for say - ing "thank you," That's a

ver - y nice thing to do. Thank you ____ for say - ing
ver - y nice thing to say. Thank you ____ for say - ing

"thank you," And you're wel - come, too. In a
"thank you," Yes, in ev - 'ry way. It's a

world that's oh, so bus - y, im - per - son - al and
thing we should re - mem - ber, and not for - get to

tough, There're two words like "thank you," that's

nev - er said quite e - nough. So, say, So,

thank you ___ for say-ing "thank you" to - day. ___

Student 12: We have a special day that's set aside for friendship and love.

Student 13: Everybody knows what that day is!

Student 14: Of course! It's Valentine's Day.

I Like You

Words and Music by Carmino Ravosa

I like you, — I like you, — I real-ly like you, — I like you, — I like you, — I real-ly do. I like you, — I like you, — I real-ly like you, — I like you, — I like you, — I real-ly do.

If you like me too, please let me know. — If you don't, then please tell me so. — I like you, — I like you, — I real-ly like you, — I like you, — I like you, — I real-ly do

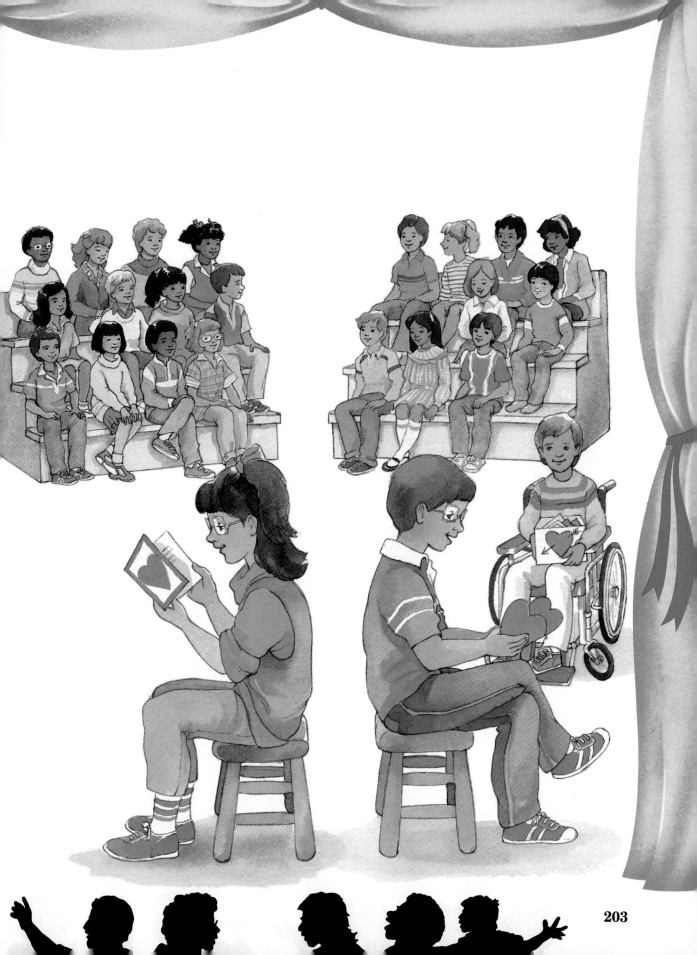

Student 15: Someone once said, "Love doesn't make the world go round, but it makes the ride worthwhile." We disagree! We think that love *does* make the world go round.

Love Makes the World Go Round

Words and Music by Carmino Ravosa

Love makes the world go round, _____
Love makes the world go round, _____

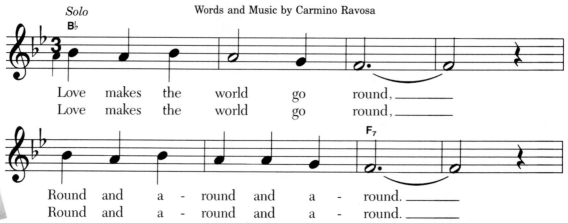

Round and a - round and a - round. _____
Round and a - round and a - round. _____

204

It makes you feel, It makes you real, Love makes the
It can't be taught, Bar - gained or bought,

1.
world go round.

2.
world go round.

D7
Love can real-ly make you feel that you're a bet-ter per - son,

G MIN

C7
And when you're in love you real - ly know you are.

F7

Chorus
Bb
Love makes the world go round,

F7
Round and a - round and a - round.

It makes you feel, It makes you real,

Solo Last Time
rit. last time
Bb a tempo
D.S.
Love makes the world go round.

Student 16: Robert Frost said, "Earth's the right place for love. I don't know where it's likely to go better."

Student 17: And I say, "Go out and love others, and have a good day."

Student 16: Have a good day! How many times have you heard that expression? Here's what *we* mean by "Have a good day!"

Have a Good Day

Words and Music by Carmino Ravosa

Have a good day, _____ Make it worth-while, _____

Go out and laugh, ___ Go out and sing, ___ Go out and smile. _____

Greeter: Well, that's our play—our songs and our message. We hope you liked it. We enjoyed doing it for you. Oh, and one more thing. When you're feeling pessimistic, or angry, or bitter—say to yourself, "Only love is spoken here!"

Jan	1 2 3 4 5 6	Jul	1 2 3 4 5 6
7 8 9 10 11 12 13 14 15		7 8 9 10 11 12 13 14 15
16 17 18 19 20 21 22 23 24		16 17 18 19 20 21 22 23 24
25 26 27 28 29 30 31		25 26 27 28 29 30 31
Feb	1 2 3 4 5 6	Aug	1 2 3 4 5 6
7 8 9 10 11 12 13 14 15		7 8 9 10 11 12 13 14 15
16 17 18 19 20 21 22 23 24		16 17 18 19 20 21 22 23 24
25 26 27 28		25 26 27 28 29 30 31
Mar	1 2 3 4 5 6	Sep	1 2 3 4 5 6
7 8 9 10 11 12 13 14 15		7 8 9 10 11 12 13 14 15
16 17 18 19 20 21 22 23 24		16 17 18 19 20 21 22 23 24
25 26 27 28 29 30 31		25 26 27 28 29 30
Apr	1 2 3 4 5 6	Oct	1 2 3 4 5 6
7 8 9 10 11 12 13 14 15		7 8 9 10 11 12 13 14 15
16 17 18 19 20 21 22 23 24		16 17 18 19 20 21 22 23 24
25 26 27 28 29 30		25 26 27 28 29 30 31
May	1 2 3 4 5 6	Nov	1 2 3 4 5 6
7 8 9 10 11 12 13 14 15		7 8 9 10 11 12 13 14 15
16 17 18 19 20 21 22 23 24		16 17 18 19 20 21 22 23 24
25 26 27 28 29 30		25 26 27 28 29 30
Jun	1 2 3 4 5 6	Dec	1 2 3 4 5 6
7 8 9 10 11 12 13 14 15		7 8 9 10 11 12 13 14 15
16 17 18 19 20 21 22 23 24		16 17 18 19 20 21 22 23 24
25 26 27 28 29 30		25 26 27 28 29 30 31

SING AND CELEBRATE

Sweet Land of Liberty

The words of "America" are set to a melody that has lived for many years. No one knows where the tune came from, but many people have used it— the Germans, the Swiss, the French. Great Britain's national anthem has the same melody.

America 9

Traditional Melody   Words by Samuel Francis Smith

1. My coun - try! 'tis of thee, Sweet land of lib - er - ty, Of thee I sing; Land where my fa - thers died, Land of the Pil - grims' pride, From ev - 'ry __ moun - tain - side Let __ free - dom ring!

2. My native country, thee, Land of the noble free,
   Thy name I love;
   I love thy rocks and rills, Thy woods and templed hills;
   My heart with rapture thrills Like that above.

3. Let music swell the breeze, And ring from all the trees
   Sweet Freedom's song;
   Let mortal tongues awake, Let all that breathe partake,
   Let rocks their silence break, The sound prolong.

4. Our fathers' God, to Thee, Author of liberty,
   To Thee we sing;
   Long may our land be bright With Freedom's holy light;
   Protect us by Thy might, Great God, our King!

Charles Ives, an American composer, used the melody of "America" in one of his compositions.

Listen to Ives' *Variations on "America"* arranged for symphony orchestra.

Variations on "America" .... **Ives**

A Nation's Strength

Not gold, but only man can make
   A people great and strong;
Men who, for truth and honor's sake,
   Stand fast and suffer long.

Brave men who work while others sleep,
   Who dare while others fly—
They build a nation's pillars deep
   And lift them to the sky.

Ralph Waldo Emerson

From Sea to Shining Sea

On a beautiful day in 1893, Katharine Lee Bates stood on the top of Colorado's Pikes Peak and looked for miles in every direction. She seemed to be seeing all of America—mountains, valleys, wide prairies. It was after this experience that she wrote the poem "America, the Beautiful."

America, the Beautiful

Words by Katharine Lee Bates   Music by Samuel A. Ward

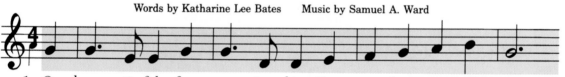

1. O beau-ti-ful for spa-cious skies, For am-ber waves of grain,

For pur-ple moun-tain maj-es-ties A-bove the fruit-ed plain!

A-mer-i-ca! A-mer-i-ca! God shed His grace on thee

And crown thy good with broth-er-hood From sea to shin-ing sea!

2. O beautiful for Pilgrim feet, Whose stern impassioned stress
A thoroughfare for freedom beat Across the wilderness!
America! America! God mend thine ev'ry flaw,
Confirm thy soul in self control, Thy liberty in law!

3. O beautiful for patriot dream That sees beyond the years
Thine alabaster cities gleam, Undimmed by human tears!
America! America! God shed His grace on thee
And crown thy good with brotherhood From sea to shining sea!

What can you discover about the phrases in this song? The
first phrase is shown in a color box.

Countermelody for Bells or Recorder

You can use this countermelody to accompany the singing of
"America, the Beautiful."

The March King

Three Themes

Here are the beginnings of the three themes that Sousa used in *The Stars and Stripes Forever*. Try to follow each one as it is played on the recording.

Listen for the three themes on this recording of Sousa's best-known march.

The Stars and Stripes Forever .... Sousa

Sousa wrote words for this march. When you have heard the piece several times, try singing them to the melody of Theme 3 when it comes in the music.

Hurrah for the flag of the free,
May it wave as our standard forever,
The gem of the land and the sea,
The banner of all the right!
Let despots remember the day
When our fathers with mighty endeavor
Proclaimed as they marched in the fray
That by their might and by their right
It waves forever!

John Philip Sousa
1854–1932

John Philip Sousa is known as the March King of the world. He was born, and grew up, in our nation's capital—Washington, D.C. Even as a little boy, he knew he wanted to be a musician. He often went to band rehearsals with his father, who played trombone in the United States Marine Band—the official band of the President of the United States. When Sousa was 26 years old he became director of this band and wrote some of his finest marches for it.

Sousa composed more than 100 marches during his lifetime. Many of these are played today by high school, college, and community bands throughout America. *The Stars and Stripes Forever* was Sousa's favorite march—it is known all over the world.

The Flag Is Passing By

Play a drum beat on your desk as you listen to the music of
"You're a Grand Old Flag."

You're a Grand Old Flag

Words and Music by George M. Cohan

You're a grand old flag, you're a high - fly - ing flag;

And for - ev - er in peace may you wave; _____

You're the em - blem of the land I love,

The home of the free and the brave. _____

Ev - 'ry heart beats true un - der red, white, and blue,

Where there's nev - er a boast or brag; _____

But should auld ac - quaint - ance be for - got,

Keep your eye on the grand old flag. _____

The Flag Goes By

Hats off!
Along the street there comes
A blare of bugles, a ruffle of drums,
A flash of color beneath the sky:
Hats off!
The flag is passing by!

Hats off!
Along the street there comes
A blare of bugles, a ruffle of drums;
And loyal hearts are beating high:
Hats off!
The flag is passing by!

Henry Holcomb Bennett

Our National Anthem

"The Star-Spangled Banner" is performed on many occasions.
What should you do when our national anthem is played or
sung?

Can you find other phrases in the music that match the
contour of the phrases shown in the color boxes?

The Star-Spangled Banner

Music by John Stafford Smith   Words by Francis Scott Key

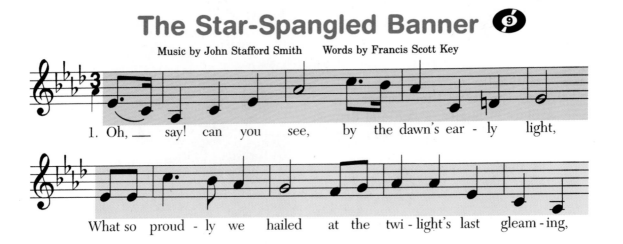

1. Oh, — say! can you see, by the dawn's ear - ly light,

What so proud - ly we hailed at the twi - light's last gleam - ing,

Whose broad stripes and bright stars, through the per - il - ous fight,

O'er the ram - parts we watched were so gal - lant - ly stream-ing?

And the rock - ets' red glare, the bombs burst - ing in air,

Gave proof through the night that our flag was still there.

Oh, say, does that _ Star-Span-gled Ban - ner _ yet _ wave _

O'er the land _ of the free and the home of the brave.

2. On the shore, dimly seen through the mists of the deep,
Where the Foe's haughty host in dread silence reposes,
What is that which the breeze, o'er the towering steep,
As it fitfully blows, half conceals, half discloses?
Now it catches the gleam of the morning's first beam,
In full glory reflected now shines on the stream;
'Tis the Star-Spangled Banner, oh, long may it wave
O'er the land of the free and the home of the brave!

3. Oh, thus be it ever when free men shall stand
Between their loved homes and the war's desolation!
Blest with vict'ry and peace, may the heav'n-rescued land
Praise the Pow'r that hath made and preserved us a nation!
Then conquer we must, for our cause it is just,
And this be our motto: "In God is our trust!"
And the Star-Spangled Banner in triumph shall wave
O'er the land of the free and the home of the brave!

Using Dynamics in Speech and Song

Think of ways of using your voice to make this Halloween song sound exciting.

Halloween 9

Words and Music by John Horman

1. You got - ta watch out ___ when the ghosts come round, ___

You got - ta watch out ___ so you won't be found, ___

'Cause if they should find you and sneak up be - hind you,

You got - ta watch out ___ when the ghosts come round. ___

2. You gotta watch out when the moon is high,
   And witches ride broomsticks across the sky,
   For if they should spy you and fly down beside you,
   You gotta watch out when the moon is high.

3. When Halloween comes around this year,
   And spooky things fill your heart with fear,
   Remember, be wary of things that are scary!
   When Halloween comes around this year.

Hallowe'en

Tonight is the night
When dead leaves fly
Like witches on switches
Across the sky.
When elf and sprite
Flit through the night
On a moony sheen.

Tonight is the night
When leaves make a sound
Like a gnome in his home
Under the ground,
When the spooks and trolls
Creep out of holes
Mossy and green.

Tonight is the night
When pumpkins stare
Through the sheaves and leaves
Everywhere,
When ghoul and ghost
And goblin host
Dance round their queen.
It's Hallowe'en!

Harry Behn

Ghosts and Goblins

What do the signs in the color boxes tell you?

Watch Out!

Words and Music by John Horman

When ghosts and gob - lins come to town, ___

And skel - e - tons all dance a - round, ___

Just pull those cov - ers o - ver your head and

then, _____ then, _____ watch out!

© 1984 John Horman

Halloween Chant

Ghosts,   Ghosts

Gob - lins, Gob - lins

Skel - e - tons, Skel - e - tons

Ooh _____

226

Partner Songs for Halloween

You got - ta watch out —— when the ghosts come round, —— You

When ghosts and gob - lins come to town, —— And

got - ta watch out —— so you won't be found, —— 'Cause

skel - e - tons all dance a - round, —— Just

if they should find you and sneak up be - hind you, You

pull the co - vers o - ver your head and

got - ta watch out —— when the ghosts come round.

then, ————————— watch out!

A Chant for Autumn

As you listen to this song, chant the first pattern softly.
This will help you feel the music moving in sets of two.

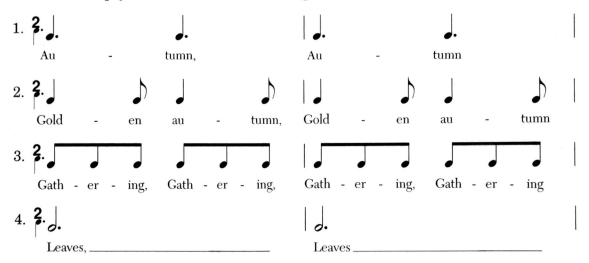

1. Au - tumn, Au - tumn

2. Gold - en au - tumn, Gold - en au - tumn

3. Gath - er - ing, Gath - er - ing, Gath - er - ing, Gath - er - ing

4. Leaves, _____ Leaves _____

Autumn

Words Anonymous   Music by John Horman

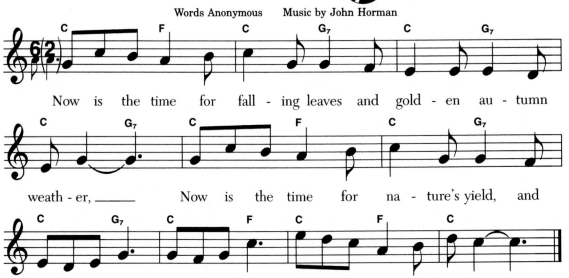

Now is the time for fall - ing leaves and gold - en au - tumn weath - er, _____ Now is the time for na - ture's yield, and gath - er - ing friends, gath - er - ing friends, Gath-er-ing friends to - geth - er. _____

© 1984 John Horman

Sing this part over and over throughout the song.

Ostinato

Now is the time.

228

Add a Bell Part

Here are two bell parts to play with "Autumn." Which one will you choose to play?

Bells

Bells

In some parts of our country, autumn is a time for raking leaves.

Gathering Leaves

Spades take up leaves
No better than spoons,
And bags full of leaves
Are light as balloons.

I make a great noise
Of rustling all day
Like rabbit and deer
Running away.

But the mountains I move
Elude my embrace,
Flowing over my arms
And into my face.

I may load and unload
Again and again
Till I fill the whole shed,
And what have I then?

Next to nothing for weight,
And since they grew duller
From contact with earth,
Next to nothing for color.

Next to nothing for use,
But a crop is a crop,
And who's to say where
The harvest shall stop?   *Robert Frost*

The First Thanksgiving

THANKSGIVING FEAST (DETAIL)
N.C. WYETH

The Pilgrims' first Thanksgiving feast took place in mid-October 1621. They were so thankful for their survival and their plentiful harvest of Indian corn that they decided to set aside a day for giving thanks. The day was filled with prayer, feasting, and merriment.

We Gather Together

English Words by Theodore Baker   Traditional Dutch Tune

p 1. We gath - er to - geth - er to ask the Lord's bless - ing;
mf 2. Be - side us to guide us, our God with us join - ing,

He chas - tens and has - tens His will to make known.
Or - dain - ing, main - tain - ing His king - dom di - vine.

230

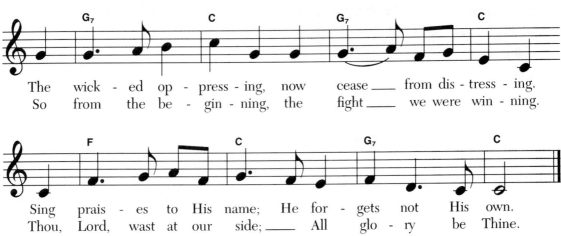

The wick - ed op - press - ing, now cease ___ from dis - tress - ing.
So from the be - gin - ning, the fight ___ we were win - ning.

Sing prais - es to His name; He for - gets not His own.
Thou, Lord, wast at our side; ___ All glo - ry be Thine.

𝆏 3. We all do extol Thee, Thou leader triumphant,
And pray that Thou still our defender wilt be.
Let Thy congregation escape tribulation.
Thy name be ever praised!
O Lord, make us free!

Harvest Festival

Sukkot is an autumn festival. It comes at the time of year when farmers cut down their full-grown wheat and get ready for the long winter.

Harvest Time

Hebrew Song   English Words by Lillian Wiedman

1. Cut the wheat, gold-en wheat, Oh, how beau-ti-ful the har-vest;
2. Pluck the grapes, pur-ple grapes, Oh, how beau-ti-ful the har-vest;
   Ha' Suk - kah, mah ya - fah u - mah tov la - she - vet bah! __

Cut the wheat, gold-en wheat, Oh, how beau-ti-ful it is!
Pluck the grapes, pur-ple grapes, Oh, how beau-ti-ful they are!
Ha' Suk - kah, mah ya - fah u - mah tov la - she - vet bah!

Follow the autoharp chord letters in the music and accompany the singing.

Add a Bell Part

232

A Family Time

Thanksgiving 🄯

Words and Music by John Horman

Tur-key and dress-ing's on the ta - ble, Sweet pump-kin pie is might-y fine,

Broth-ers and sis-ters, aunts and un-cles, Thanks-giv-ing is a fam'-ly time.

Heads we bow, hands we fold, Thank-ful prayers our hearts will hold;

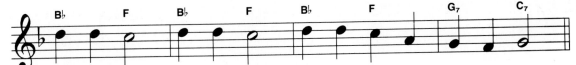

Hands and hearts, hearts and hands join to stretch a - cross the land.

© 1984 John Horman

House Blessing

Bless the four corners of this house,
    And be the lintel blessed;
And bless the heart and bless the board
    And bless each place to rest;
And bless the door that opens wide
    To stranger as to kin;
And bless each crystal window-pane
    That lets the starlight in;
And bless the rooftree overhead
    And every sturdy wall.
The peace of man, the peace of God,
    The peace of Love on all!

Arthur Guiterman

Christmas-Time in the City

Listen for the echo part in the recording of this song. In which section do you hear it—section A or section B?

Silver Bells 🄥

Words and Music by Jay Livingston and Ray Evans

1. Cit - y side-walks, bus - y side-walks dressed in hol - i - day style

In the air there's a feel - ing of Christ - mas. _____

Child-ren laugh-ing, peo-ple pass-ing, meet-ing smile af-ter smile,

And on ev' - ry street cor - ner you hear: ____

B REFRAIN

Sil - ver bells, ____ (Sil - ver bells,) Sil - ver bells, ____ (Sil - ver bells,)

It's Christ - mas time in the cit - y. ____

Ring - a - ling, ____ (Ring - a - ling,) Hear them ring, ____ (Hear them ring,)

Soon it will be Christ - mas day. ____

2. Strings of street lights, even stop lights
   blink a bright red and green,
   As the shoppers rush home with their treasures.
   Hear the snow crunch, see the kids bunch,
   this is Santa's big scene,
   And above all this bustle you hear: *Refrain*

Listen for the jingle of the sleighbells and the cracking
whip in this lively music by Leroy Anderson.
Sleigh Ride .... **Anderson**

Festival of Lights

Follow the music in your book as you listen to the recording of "O Chanukah." Can you tell when the voices are singing in unison? In Harmony?

O Chanukah

Jewish Folk Song   English Words by Judith Eisenstein

From THE GATEWAY TO JEWISH SONG, by Judith Eisenstein. Reprinted by permission of the author.

Introduction and Coda

For a performance of "O Chanukah," add an introduction at
the beginning and a coda at the end of the song.

Finger cymbals
Tambourine

Breaking the Piñata

Children in Mexico celebrate Christmas Eve in a special way. Read the words of this song to find out why this is such an exciting time of the year.

Piñata Song ⑨

(Al Quebrar la Piñata)

Christmas Song from Mexico English Words by Verne Muñoz

A
C F
In the hap - py days of Christ - mas, ____
En las no - ches de po - sa - das, ____
G7 C
Sounds of glad - ness fill the air; ____
La pi - ña - ta es lo me - jor; ____
C7 F
When it's time for the pi - ña - ta, ____
La ni - ña más re - mil - ga - da ____
G7 C
There's ex - cite - ment ev - 'ry - where. ____
Se al - bo - ro - ta con ar - dor. ____

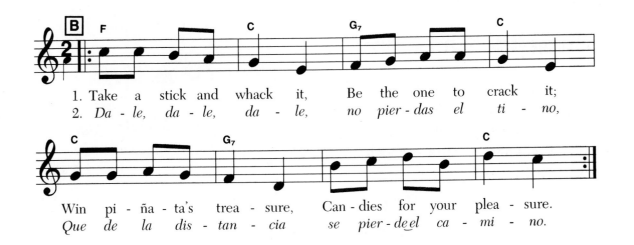

1. Take a stick and whack it, Be the one to crack it;
2. *Da - le, da - le, da - le, no pier - das el ti - no,*

Win pi - ña - ta's trea - sure, Can - dies for your plea - sure.
Que de la dis - tan - cia se pier - de el ca - mi - no.

Percussion Accompaniment for Section B

Maracas

Play throughout.

Claves

A Yuletide Carol

Long ago in the British Isles, people decorated the grey stone castle walls with boughs of holly while the yule log burned brightly.

Deck the Hall

Traditional   Old Welsh Carol

1. { Deck the hall with boughs of hol - ly,
   'Tis the sea - son to be jol - ly,
   { See the blaz - ing Yule be - fore us,
2. { Strike the harp and join the cho - rus,

Fa la la la la la la la la.

Don we now our gay ap - par - el,
Fol - low me in mer - ry meas - ure,

Fa la la la la la la la la.

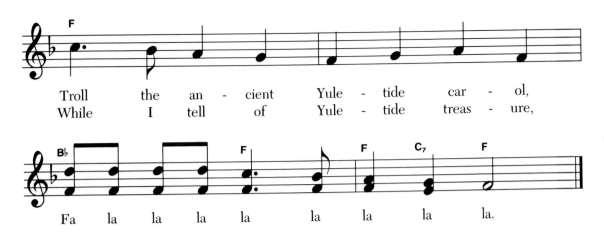

Troll the an - cient Yule - tide car - ol,
While I tell of Yule - tide treas - ure,

Fa la la la la la la la la.

3. Fast away the old year passes,
Fa la la la la la la la la.
Hail the new, ye lads and lasses,
Fa la la la la la la la la.
Sing we joyous all together,
Fa la la la la la la la la.
Heedless of the wind and weather,
Fa la la la la la la la la.

Going A-Caroling

In the first section of this song, the carolers go from door to door. What do you think they will do when they sing the refrain?

Here We Come A-Wassailing

English Carol

1. Here we come a-was-sail-ing A-mong the leaves so green;
2. We are not dai-ly beg-gars That beg from door to door;

Here we come a-wan-d'ring, So fair to be seen.
But we are neigh-bors' chil-dren, Whom you have seen be-fore.

REFRAIN

Love and joy come to you, And to you glad Christ-mas too;

And God bless you and send you a hap-py New Year,

And God send you a hap-py New Year.

3. God bless the master of this house,
   Likewise the mistress, too,
   And all the little children
   That round the table go. *Refrain*

242

Added Parts

SECTION A

Descant (Voices or bells)

Was - sail, was - sail, Was - sail, was - sail,

1. Here we come, _____ so fair _____ to be seen.
2. We are chil - dren you have seen be - fore.
3. God bless all _____ that 'round the ta - ble go.

SECTION B

Finger cymbals

Play throughout.

A Christmas Greeting

This old English greeting was sung by carolers who hoped for a treat!

We Wish You a Merry Christmas

English Carol

1. We wish you a mer-ry Christ-mas, We wish you a mer-ry Christ-mas,

We wish you a mer-ry Christ-mas, And a hap-py New Year!

2. Now bring us some figgy pudding,
   And bring it out here.

3. For we love our figgy pudding,
   So bring some out here.

4. We won't go until we get some,
   So bring some out here.

Added Parts to Sing and Play

1. We wish you, we wish you, We
2. Now bring us, now bring us, Now

wish you a hap - py New Year.
bring us, And bring it out here.

3. For we love, for we love,
   For we love, So bring some out here.

4. We won't go, we won't go,
   We won't go, So bring some out here.

Bells

246

Sing Noel

In France, carols are called *noels*. Pat the steady beat on an imaginary drum as you listen to this old French noel.

Pat-A-Pan

Early Burgundian French Carol   English Words by Rosemary Jacques

1. Wil - lie, bring your fin - est drum; Rob - in, take your flute and come; Play a joy - ful song of praise, *Tu - re - lu - re - lu,* *pat - a - pat - a - pan,* Play a joy - ful song of praise On this won - drous day of days.

2. Long ago on Christmas morn
When the holy Child was born,
Shepherds from the fields did come,
Turelurelu, patapatapan,
Shepherds from the fields did come
Playing on their pipe and drum.

3. So 'tis fitting on this day
That on instruments we play,
Like the humble shepherd men,
Turelurelu, patapatapan,
Like the humble shepherd men
Who were there in Bethlehem.

Pat-a-Pan Accompaniments

Bells

Recorder

Drum

Finger cymbals

Twelve Gifts

Follow the music as you listen to this cumulative song. Try not to get lost!

The Twelve Days of Christmas 🔟

Version of Frederick Austin   Old English Folk Song

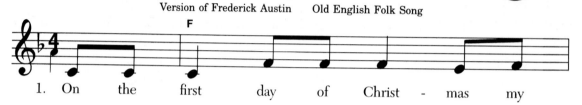

1. On the first day of Christ - mas my

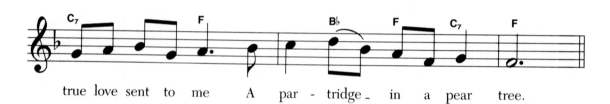

true love sent to me A par - tridge in a pear tree.

2. On the second day of Christ - mas my true love sent to me
3. On the third day of Christ - mas my true love sent to me
4. On the fourth day of Christ - mas my true love sent to me

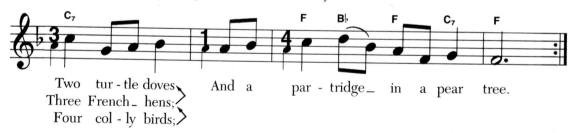

Two tur - tle doves And a par - tridge in a pear tree.
Three French hens;
Four col - ly birds;

5. On the fifth day of Christ - mas my true love sent to me

By permission of Novello & Co., Ltd.

8. On the eighth day . . .
   Eight maids a-milking; . . .

10. On the tenth day . . .
    Ten lords a-leaping; . . .

9. On the ninth day . . .
   Nine ladies dancing; . . .

11. On the eleventh day . . .
    Eleven pipers piping; . . .

12. On the twelfth day of Christmas
    My true love sent to me
    Twelve drummers drumming; Eleven pipers piping;
    Ten lords a-leaping; Nine ladies dancing;
    Eight maids a-milking; Seven swans a-swimming;
    Six geese a-laying; Five golden rings;
    Four colly birds; Three French hens;
    Two turtle doves and a partridge in a pear tree.

Three Kings' Day

If you were to spend Christmas
in Puerto Rico you would say
Merry Christmas this way:
Felices Pascuas!

Children in Puerto Rico receive
gifts on Three Kings' Day, which is
celebrated on the sixth of January.

Three Kings 🔟

Puerto Rican Carol   English Version by Aura Kontra

1. Three _ kings are com - ing, _ how ho - ly __ they are,

Three _ kings are com - ing, _ how ho - ly __ they are,

In good faith we'll greet them, _ for they've trav - eled far.

In good faith we'll greet them, _ for they've trav - eled far.

2. Carefully they follow a star shining bright, *(2 times)*
   Weary steps move slowly, and cold is the night. *(2 times)*

3. It is time to leave you, we're going away, *(2 times)*
   Happy, happy New Year to all here today. *(2 times)*

250

Here are the Spanish words of the song. Try following
them as you listen to the recording. You might want to try
singing along.

1. Los tres Santos Reyes los tres. (2 times)
   Los saludaremos con divina fe. (2 times)

2. Llegan con cautela, la estrella los guía. (2 times)
   Se sienten sus pasos en la noche fría. (2 times)

3. Señores, adiós, porque ya nos vamos, (2 times)
   Todos los presentes pasen feliz año. (2 times)

Accompaniment Patterns

These patterns can be played throughout the song.

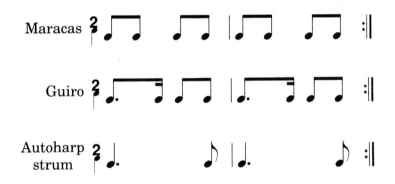

You can sing this countermelody. You can also play it on bells
or recorder.

Can You Read This?

You know that this is music, but do you know how it sounds?

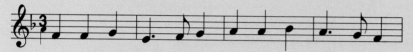

You know that these are words, but do you know how they sound?

My country, 'tis of thee
Sweet land of liberty,
Of thee I sing. . .

You know how the words sound because you have learned to read words. You understand the symbols (letters) that stand for the sounds of spoken language.

You can read music when you learn to understand the symbols that stand for the sounds in music.

Musical symbols can tell us the rhythm of the music.

Clap this pattern: 1.

Clap this pattern: 2.

Added musical symbols tell us more about the rhythm.

Clap this pattern: 3.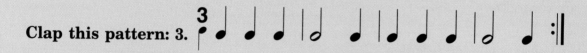

When we add the five-line staff, we can tell whether the music goes UP . . . or goes DOWN . . . or STAYS THE SAME:

Can You Read a Melody? Each of the following melodies will harmonize with a song in your book.

A Melody that Moves by Step. Sing this tonal pattern that goes up and then down:

4.

A Melody With Repeated Tones. This pattern uses repeated notes. It moves up once, but mostly it stays the same:

5.

A Longer "Ostinato" Melody. This pattern does all three things. It moves up, moves down, and repeats a note:

6.

A Longer Melody With a Repeating Pattern. This longer melody is actually made out of a shorter repeated pattern:

7.

A Melody that Moves Upward and Downward: When music moves up or down in pitch, it sometimes moves by "step." That means it goes to a note that is just next to it, up or down:

8.

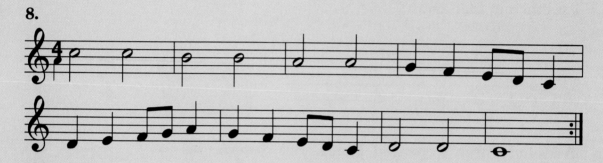

A Melody With Leaps. Sometimes the melody will move upward or downward by "leap." That means it will skip over notes just next to it and jump to a note further away:

9.

A Melody With Wider Leaps. Some leaps jump further than others.

10.

A Melody With Steps and Leaps. Usually a melody is a combination of steps and leaps:

11.

Repeat

A Longer, More Complicated Melody. Musical patterns that repeat are easier to hear and easier to read. We can find some parts that are the same, but changes in the pattern make music more interesting:

12.

A Countermelody to a Very Familiar Song. Even when the patterns of a melody seem to be very different, there are still things we can see and hear which are nearly the same:

13.

A Melody that Turns Upside Down. The first half of this
melody leaps upward. The second half begins by leaping
downward. The last line is a "sequence."

14.

**A Melody With an Uneven Rhythm and a Very Large
Leap.** Often very wide leaps are not as difficult as they
look:

15.

A Melody With Even and Uneven Rhythms. Reading
music can be like following a road. Sometimes there are signs
telling us which way to go:

16.

A Melody that Keeps Changing Direction. Sometimes
reading music can be like following a *winding* road. We have
to be careful to make turns in the right direction:

17.

Playing the Autoharp

The picture shows you
the correct position for
playing the autoharp.

Two-Chord Accompaniment

Follow these directions to play a two-chord
accompaniment.
- Place your left index finger on the button marked *F*.
- Place your left middle finger on the button marked C_7.
- Look at the chord pattern below. It shows when to press
  each button.
- As you press the buttons, use your right hand to strum the
  strings. Make each strum last for two beats.

You can use the F and C_7 chord pattern to accompany the
song "Mary Ann," page 60.

Three-Chord Accompaniment

Follow these directions to play a three-chord accompaniment.

- Place your left index finger on the button marked *C*.
- Place your left middle finger on the button marked G_7.
- Place your left ring finger on the button marked *F*.
- Look at the chord pattern below. It shows when to press each button.
- As you press the buttons, use your right hand to strum the strings. Make each strum last for two beats.

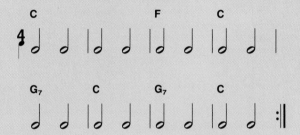

You can use the C, G_7, and F chord pattern to accompany the song "Hey Dum Diddeley Dum," page 174.

Follow the Chord Names

Try playing an accompaniment for other two- and three-chord songs. The chord names in the music will tell you which buttons to press and when to change from one chord to another.

- Clementine, page 18
- Old Texas, page 46
- La Cucaracha, page 62
- Some Folks, page 12
- Oh, Susanna, page 14
- So Long, page 22

Playing the Recorder

Using your left hand, cover the holes shown in the first diagram.

Cover the tip of the mouthpiece with your lips. Blow gently as you whisper "daah." You will be playing *B*.

When you can play B, A, and G, you will be able to play melody 1.

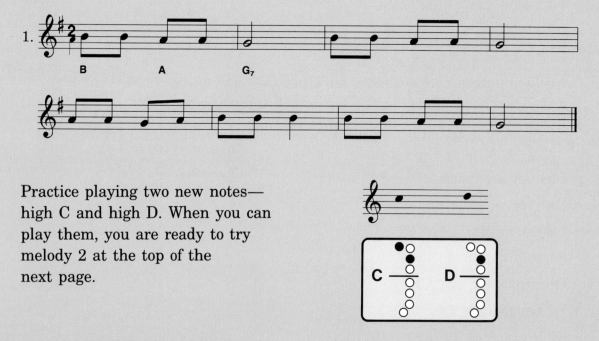

Practice playing two new notes—high C and high D. When you can play them, you are ready to try melody 2 at the top of the next page.

2.

Here are four new notes to practice. When you can play them, you will be ready to try melody 3.

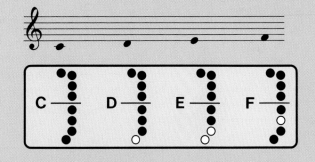

3.

Using the notes you have learned so far, you will be able to play some of the songs in your book. Try one of these.

- Breezes Are Blowing, page 24
- Sarasponda, page 114
- Barges, page 32
- Winter Fun, page 108

Here are two new notes to practice—F♯ and B♭. When you can play them, you will be ready to try one of the songs listed below.

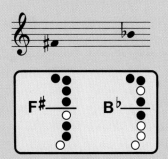

- Chairs to Mend, page 53
- Music Alone Shall Live, page 113
- Mary Ann, page 60
- Goodnight, page 163

The Sound Bank

Bassoon A large, tube-shaped wooden wind instrument with a double reed. (p. 143)
• Lower notes on the bassoon can be gruff or comical. Higher notes are the same notes children sing, and these are softer, sweeter and more gentle-sounding.

Cello A large wooden string instrument. The player sits with the cello between his knees and reaches around the front to play it. (p. 141)
• The cello has a low, rich-sounding voice which can also go up to notes children sing.

Clarinet A wind instrument shaped like a long cylinder. It is usually made of wood and has a reed in the mouthpiece. (p. 143)
• Low notes on the clarinet are soft and hollow. The middle notes are open and bright, and the highest notes are thin and piercing.

Flute A small metal instrument shaped like a pipe. The player holds the flute sideways and blows across an open mouthpiece. (p. 143)
• The flute's voice is pure, clear and sweet. Its low notes are the same ones children sing, but it can also go very high.

French Horn A medium-size instrument made of coiled brass tubing. At one end is a large "bell." The player holds the horn on his lap and keeps one hand inside the bell. (p. 145)
• The sound of the horn is very mellow. It can go higher and lower than children's voices, but its best notes are the same ones children sing best.

Oboe A slender wooden wind instrument with a double reed. (p. 143)
• In its low voice the oboe can sound mysterious and "oriental." These are the notes children sing. When it goes higher the sound is thin and sweet.

String Bass The largest string instrument, the one with the lowest voice. A string bass is usually taller than a person. The player must stand or sit on a high stool. (p. 141)
• The string bass has a deep, dark voice. Sometimes it is gruff, sometimes mellow.

Timpani Large pot-shaped drums, also called "Kettledrums." Unlike most drums, they can be tuned to notes of the scale. The player can use several drums and play a tune. (p. 147)
• The timpani can sound like a heartbeat or a roll of thunder. Its voice can be a loud "boom," a quiet "thump" or a distant rumble, depending on how it is played.

Trombone A large brass instrument with the loudest voice in the orchestra. It has tubing, a "bell," and a long, curved "slide." (p. 145)
• The trombone can be loud and brilliant, but its soft voice is mellow. It can play the notes children sing, but also go much lower.

Trumpet The smallest brass instrument, but one with a big sound. (p. 145)
• The trumpet's voice can be loud and bright, but can also sound warm and sweet. Most of its notes are the same as children sing.

Tuba The largest brass instrument, the one with the lowest voice. (p. 145)
• The tuba's low notes are deep and "dark" sounding. The higher ones are hearty and warm.

Viola A wooden string instrument played like a violin. (p. 141)
• The viola's voice is similar to the violin's, but deeper, richer and "darker."

Violin A wooden string instrument held under the player's chin. (p. 141)
• The violin has many different voices. It plays the notes children sing, but can also go much higher. A good player can create many unusual and interesting sounds on the violin.

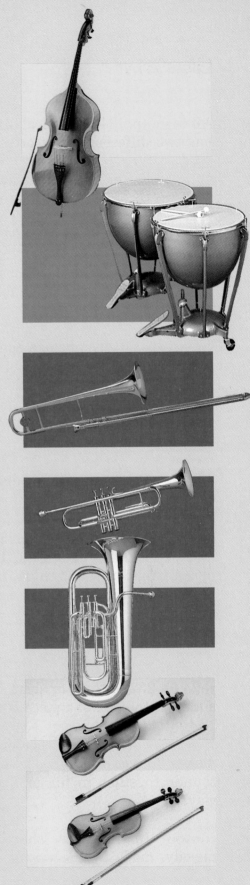

Reference Bank 263

Glossary

AB form (p. 124) A musical plan that has two different parts, or sections.

ABA form (p. 126) A musical plan that has three sections. The first and last sections are the same. The middle section is different.

accompaniment (p. 42) Music that supports the sound of the featured performer(s).

ballad (p. 20) In music, a song that tells a story.

band (p. 148) A balanced group of instruments consisting of woodwinds, brass, and percussion.

beat (p. 12) A repeating pulse that can be felt in some music.

brass (p. 144) A group of wind instruments, including trumpets, French horns, trombones, and tubas, used in bands and orchestras.

chorus (p. 136) A large group of singers.

coda (p. 237) A "tail" or short section added at the end of a piece of music.

composer (p. 96) A person who makes up pieces of music by putting sounds together in his or her own way.

contour (p. 110) The "shape" of a melody, made by the way it moves upward and downward in steps and leaps, and by repeated tones.

countermelody (p. 65) A melody that is played or sung at the same time as another melody.

descant (p. 122) A countermelody whose main function is to decorate the main tune, often soaring above the melody of the song.

duet (p. 136) A composition written for two performers.

dynamics (p. 163) The loudness and softness of sound (*f, mf, p, mp, <, >, and so on*).

form (p. 124) The overall plan of a piece of music.

harmony (p. 17) Two or more different tones sounding at the same time.

introduction (p. 237) In a song, music played before the singing begins.

leap (p. 107) To move from one tone to another, skipping over the tones in between.

lullaby (p. 181) A quiet song, often sung when rocking a child to sleep.

measure (p. 87) A grouping of beats set off by bar lines.

melody (p. 98) A line of single tones that move upward, downward, or repeat.

melody pattern (p. 59) An arrangement of pitches into a small grouping, usually occurring often in a piece.

meter (p. 80) The way the beats of music are grouped, often in sets of two or in sets of three.

mood (p. 164) The feeling that a piece of music gives. The *mood* of a lullaby is quiet and gentle.

orchestra (p. 138) A balanced group of instruments consisting of strings, woodwinds, brass, and percussion.

ostinato (p. 114) A rhythm or melody pattern that repeats.

partner songs (p. 41) Two or more different songs that can be sung at the same time to create harmony.

percussion (p. 21) A group of pitched or unpitched instruments that are played by striking with mallets, beaters, and so on, or by shaking.

phrase (p. 43) A musical "sentence." Each *phrase* expresses one thought.

refrain (p. 17) The part of a song that repeats, using the same melody and words.

repeated tones (p. 98) Two or more tones in a row that have the same sound.

rhythm pattern (p. 59) A group of long and short sounds. Some rhythm patterns have even sounds. Others have uneven sounds.

rondo (p. 128) A musical form in which a section is repeated, with contrasting sections in between (such as ABACA).

round (p. 26) A follow-the-leader process in which all sing the same melody but start at different times.

sequence (p. 113) The repetition of a melody pattern at a higher or lower pitch level.

shanties (p. 29) Sailors' work songs.

steady beat (p. 78) Regular pulses.

step (p. 107) To move from one tone to another without skipping tones in between.

solo (p. 132) Music for a single singer or player, often with an accompaniment.

strings (p. 140) A term used to refer to stringed instruments that are played by bowing, plucking, or strumming.

strong beat (p. 87) The first beat in a measure.

tempo (p. 167) The speed of the beat in music.

texture (p. 162) The way melody and harmony go together: a melody alone, two or more melodies together, or a melody with chords.

theme (p. 89) An important melody that occurs several times in a piece of music.

trio (p. 136) Any composition for three voices or instruments, each having a separate part.

woodwinds (p. 142) A term used to refer to wind instruments, now or originally made of wood.

Classified Index

Reference Bank   267

Song Index

Acknowledgments

Credit and appreciation are due publishers and copyright owners for use of the following.

"The Flag Goes By" used with the kind permission of Martha Trumble Bennett.

"Gathering Leaves" from THE POETRY OF ROBERT FROST edited by Edward Connery Lathem. Copyright 1923, © 1969 by Holt, Rinehart and Winston. Copyright 1951 by Robert Frost. Reprinted by permission of Holt, Rinehart and Winston and the estate of Robert Frost.

"Hallowe'en" and "Spring Rain" from THE LITTLE HILL by Harry Behn, copyright 1949 by Harry Behn; renewed 1977 by Alice L. Behn. Reprinted by permission of Harcourt Brace Jovanovich, Inc.

"Harvest" by M. M. Hutchinson from LET'S ENJOY POETRY by Rosalind Hughes © 1961. Published by Houghton Mifflin. Rights to book now controlled by J. M. Dent and Sons, Ontario, Canada.

"House Blessing" from DEATH AND GENERAL PUTNAM AND 101 OTHER POEMS by Arthur Guiterman. Copyright 1935 by E. P. Dutton. Reprinted by permission of Louise H. Sclone.

"I Am Crying from Thirst" from THE WHISPERING WIND. Used by permission of the author.

"Little Talk" from THAT'S WHY by Alan Fisher Publisher; Thomas Nelson & Sons, 1946. Copyright renewed 1974. Used with permission.

"The Mysterious Cat" reprinted with permission of Macmillan Publishing Company from COLLECTED POEMS by Vachel Lindsay. Copyright 1914 by Macmillan Publishing Company, renewed 1942 by Elizabeth C. Lindsay.

"Other Children" by permission of Helen Wing.

"Something Told the Wild Geese" reprinted with permission of Macmillan Publishing Company from BRANCHES GREEN by Rachel Field. Copyright 1934 by Macmillan Publishing Company, renewed 1962 by Arthur S. Pederson.

"Ring Around the World" from ALL THROUGH THE YEAR by Annette Wynne (J.B. Lippencott Co.). Copyright 1932, 1960 by Annette Wynne. By permission of Harper & Row, Publishers, Inc.

Picture Credits

Contributing Artists: Katherine Ace, Patti Boyd, Eulala Connor, Lydia Halverson, Gary Lippencott, E. J. Miles, Nancy Munger, Cathy Pauia, Andrea Vuocola, David Wisniewski.

Photographs: 10: Silver Burdett. 14: Robin Hood Photography. 22: Brown Brothers. 25: R. Erdoes/Shostal Associates. 26: Carroll Seghers II/Leo deWys, Inc. 30: Bettmann Archive. 34: Granger Collection. 41: J. R. Eyerman for Silver Burdett. 57: Martha Swope. 58: H. Frauca/Shostal Associates. 61: Silver Burdett. 65: (c) Sven O. Lindblad/Photo Researchers, Inc. 67, 69, 82: Silver Burdett. 96–97: Victoria Beller-Smith for Silver Burdett. 110: Craig Aurness/West Light. 132: From the 20th Century Fox Release THE KING AND I (c) 1956 20th Century Fox Film Corporation. All Rights Reserved. 135: Culver Pictures. 137: Silver Burdett, Courtesy Westminster Choir College, Princeton, NJ. 138–139: Robert Lightfoot for Silver Burdett. 140: Silver Burdett. 141: Silver Burdett; instruments courtesy of Dorn & Kirschner Band & Instrument Co., Union, NJ. 142: Silver Burdett. 143: John Bacchus for Silver Burdett; instruments courtesy of Dorn & Kirschner Band & Instrument Co., Union, NJ. 144: Silver Burdett. 145: Silver Burdett, instruments courtesy of Dorn & Kirschner Band & Instrument Co., Union, NJ. 146: Silver Burdett. 147: Silver Burdett, Instruments courtesy Morris School District, Board of Education. 148–149: Silver Burdett, Rutgers University Concert Band. 168–169: Silver Burdett, Courtesy St. Peter's Episcopal Church, Morristown, NJ. 173: (c) P. Larsen/Photo Researchers, Inc. 174, 175: Dan De Wilde for Silver Burdett. 210: Karl Kummels/Shostal Associates. 214: Rosemary Scott/Taurus Photos. 217: 1. (c) Guy Gillette/Photo Researchers, Inc.; r. (c) Porterfield-Chickering/Photo Researchers, Inc. 220: Joe Tomala, Jr./Bruce Coleman. 222: Paul J. Sutton/Duomo Photography. 234: (c) Russ Kinne/Photo Researchers, Inc. 236: Silver Burdett, Courtesy Dan Mullay. 243: John O'Connor/Monkmeyer Press. 244, 258, 260: Silver Burdett. Sound Bank: Silver Burdett and John Bacchus; instruments courtesy of Dorn & Kirschner Band & Instrument Co., Union, NJ and Morris School District, Board of Education.

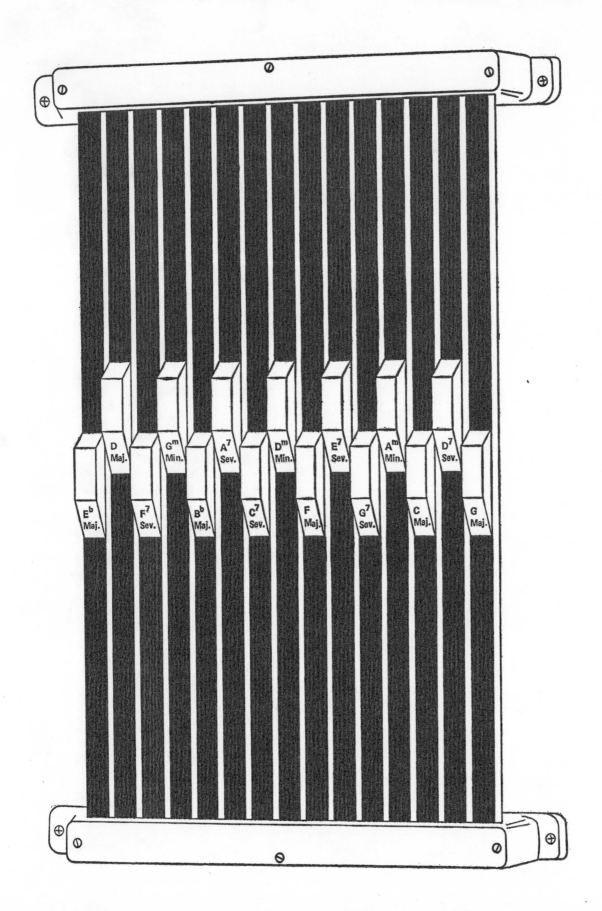